THE
ABCs
OF
Gold
Investing

Protecting Your Wealth Through Private Gold Ownership

Michael J. Kosares

ADDICUS BOOKS

An Addicus Nonfiction Book

Web Site: www.AddicusBooks.com

ISBN# 1-886039-29-1

Cover design by George Foster

This publication is sold with the understanding that the Publisher or Author is not engaged in rendering legal, accounting or other professional service. If legal advice or other expert assistance is required, the services of a competent professional person should be sought. The Author disclaims any personal liability, loss, or risk incurred as a consequence of the use and application, either directly or indirectly, of any advice or information presented herein.

Library of Congress Cataloging-in-Publication Data

Kosares, Michael J.,
  The ABCs of gold investing : protecting your wealth through private gold ownership / by Michael J. Kosares.
    p. cm.
  Includes index.
  ISBN 1-886039-29-1
  1. Gold—United States—Purchasing. 2. Investments—United States. I. Title.
HG295.U6K67 1997   96-39732
                  332.63—dc21   CIP

Printed in the United States of America

10 9 8 7 6 5 4

*To my family—Nancy, Jonathan and Andrea—
because not all that glitters is gold...*

Contents

Acknowledgments

The following organizations played an instrumental role in assisting me with the research for this book: Gold Fields Mineral Services, Ltd., of London, England, United Kingdom; the World Gold Council of New York; The Gold Institute; the United States Mint; the Austrian Mint; the Royal Canadian Mint; the Gold Corp. of Australia; the South African Chamber of Mines; the American Numismatic Association; the Mexican Consulate in Denver, Colorado; and the Industry Council for Tangible Assets. For their prompt and complete support, I owe them a huge debt of gratitude. Without them, *The ABCs of Gold Investing* would have remained an unrealized dream.

Introduction

This book is a distillation of nearly a quarter century of experience working with private investors interested in adding gold to their investment portfolios. It is not another "get rich quick" or "beat the market" treatise. Instead, it addresses a more practical concern—how to protect your wealth during what many believe are increasingly dangerous times for the average investor. Sensational returns or making the quick turn for big profits is not what gold investing is all about. Gold has to do with medium- to long-term asset preservation—weathering the storm and having something left after the dust clears. Since the investor is essentially trading an inherently unstable and depreciating form of money for one that has withstood the test of time, incorporating gold into your investment plan is among the more conservative strategies you can undertake. I often counsel investors that purchasing gold is not "investing" at all. In reality, you are simply replacing one form of money in your savings plan with another.

During the past year or two, interest in gold has accelerated to levels not seen since the 1970s. There are good reasons for this, not the least of which is a sense that there are some deep, underlying problems in the U.S. economy. Now, with *The ABCs of Gold Investing*, I offer practical knowledge required to make an informed decision about gold. These are indeed uncertain times. Perhaps gold can offer you what it has offered countless others over the centuries—solid, unassailable protection against the gathering storm.

Michael J. Kosares
Cuchara, Colorado

*Indeed there can be no other criterion, no other standard
than gold. Yes, gold which never changes,
which can be shaped into ingots, bars, coins,
which has no nationality and which is eternally
and universally accepted as the unalterable
fiduciary value par excellence.*

—Charles de Gaulle

1

A is for...
Asset Preservation: Why Americans Need Gold

> *The possession of gold has ruined fewer men than the lack of it.*
> —*Thomas Bailey Aldrich*

The incident is one of the most memorable of my career. Never before or since has the value of gold in preserving assets been made so abundantly clear to me.

It was the mid-1970s. The United States was finally extricating itself from the conflict in South Vietnam. Thousands of South Vietnamese had fled their embattled homeland rather than face the vengeance of the rapidly advancing Communist forces. In my Denver office, a couple from South Vietnam who had been part of that exodus sat across from me. They had come to sell their gold. In broken English the man told me the story of how he and his wife had escaped the fall of Saigon and certain reprisal by North Vietnamese troops. They got out with nothing more than a few personal belongings and the small cache of gold he now spread before me on my desk. His eyes widened as he explained why they were lucky to have survived those last fearful days of the South Vietnamese republic. They had scrambled onto a fishing boat and had sailed into the South China Sea, where they were rescued by the U.S. Navy. These were Vietnamese "boat people," survivors of the final chapter in the tragedy of Indochina. Now they were about to redeem their life savings in gold so that they could start a new business in the United States.

Their gold, wrapped in rice paper, was a type called Kim Thanh. These are the commonly traded units in Hong Kong and throughout the Far East. Kim Thanh weigh about 1.2 troy ounces, or a *tael*, as it is called in the Orient. They look like thick gold leaf rectangles about 3 or 4 inches long, 1 1/2 to 2 inches wide, and a few millimeters deep. Kim Thanh are embossed with Oriental characters describing weight and purity. As a gesture to the Occident, they are stamped in the center with the words *OR PUR*, pure gold.

It wasn't much gold—about 30 ounces—but it might as well have been a ton. The couple considered themselves very fortunate to have escaped with this small hoard of gold. They thanked me profusely for buying it. As we talked about Vietnam and their future in the United States, I couldn't help but become caught up in their enthusiasm for the future. These resilient, hard-working, thrifty people now had a new lease on life. When they left my office that day, there was little doubt in my mind that they would be successful in their new life. It was rewarding to know that gold could do this for them. It was satisfying to know that I had helped them in this small way.

I kept those golden Kim Thanh for many years. They became something of a symbol for me—a reminder of the power and importance of gold. Today, when economic problems have begun to signal deeper, more fundamental concerns for the United States, I still remember that Vietnamese couple and how important gold can be to a family's future. Had the couple escaped with South Vietnamese paper money instead of gold, I could have done nothing for them. There was no exchange rate for the South Vietnamese currency because there was no longer a South Vietnam! Wisely, they had converted their savings to gold long before the helicopters lifted U.S. diplomats off the roof of the American embassy in 1975.

Why Americans Need Gold

Over the years, I have come to understand and appreciate the many important uses of gold—cultural, artistic, economic and industrial. Gold is unsurpassed for jewelry and as a high-tech conductor of electricity. Gold has medical applications in dentistry and in treating diseases from arthritis to cancer. Gold plating is used in computers and in many other space-age technologies. All of these pale, though, in light of gold's ancient function as money. As an asset of last resort, gold makes its most important contribution to the general welfare. Through the many economic debacles in human history runs one common thread: those who financially survive do so because they own gold.

In recent years, gold has regained its glitter among American investors. This renewed interest in gold is not so much a hedge against the devastation of war but instead against something much more subtle—the potential destruction of wealth from an international collapse of the dollar and a subsequent economic breakdown. The telltale symptoms of a currency and an economy in stress dominate the U.S. financial and political scene. The litany is familiar: massive federal government deficits, a burdensome and virtually unpayable national debt, a rapidly growing foreign-held debt, unsustainable levels of private indebtedness, confiscatory taxation, high structural inflation rates, and declining productivity across the board. However, only a handful understand that these problems are deeply rooted and that they directly affect the viability and value of investment portfolios for all Americans.

These problems have not suddenly appeared on the horizon and demanded attention. They have been with us for a long time, and they have been steadily eating away at the foundation of the American economy: the value of the U.S. dollar. Many are hoping this deteriorating situation will simply disappear. But most of us know that is unlikely. More likely, the situation will worsen.

Just as our bodies adjust to and become inured to the cold, so too our minds have become dulled by the repetitive, steady drumbeat of statistics that prove our economy is in crisis (Figure 1).

1) In 1970, the budget deficit was a meager $2.8 billion. By 1994, it had reached $203 billion—71 times the 1970 figure.

Figure 1. Disturbing Trends 1970 to Present

Item	1970	Present	Change
Population	205 million	260 million	+12.7%
Median Income (Annual)	$9,867	$36,959	+374.5%
Federal Taxes Collected (Annual)	$192.8	$1,346	+698.1%
Social Security Expenditures (Annual)	$30.27	$336.1	+1,110%
Social Program Spending (Annual)	$75.35	$926	+1,229%
Military Spending (Annual)	$81.69	$271.6	+332.4%
Budget Deficit (Annual)	$2.85	$203	+7,122%
Accumulated Federal Debt	$436	$5,500	+1,215.6
Accumulated Federal Debt as % of GDP	38.7%	70.6%	
Interest on Fed. Debt as % of Taxes Collected	7.4%	17.3%	
Merchandise Trade Deficit (Annual)	Balanced	$166.364	+16,636%
Consumer Price Index (Cumulative)	38.8	148.2	+382%
Money Supply (M3)	$1,989	$4,553	+229%
Purchasing Power of Dollar (Cumulative)	$1	26 cents	-74%
Total World Gold Stock	75,000 tons	110,000 tons	+46%

Monetary Figures in Billions

2) In 1970, the accumulated federal debt was $436 billion. Now it is $5.5 trillion. This figure does not include so-called "off budget" items, another $300 billion in 1996.

3) Exports and imports were roughly balanced in 1970. In 1995, the trade deficit was $105 billion. Few can

remember the last time the United States ran a trade surplus (1975).

4) In the process, the United States has gone from being the greatest creditor nation on earth to being the world's greatest debtor nation. Foreign-held debt increased by nearly 20 percent in 1996 alone. The problem of foreign-held debt has become so acute that some experts wonder whether the United States will be capable of pursuing its own monetary policy in the future or whether the dollar is now hostage to our foreign creditors.

5) Belying political claims that inflation is under control, the actual consumer price index has shot up 382 percent since 1970.

6) While proclaiming that the American consumer has never had it better, many politicians neglect to mention that tax collections by the government have gone up nearly 700 percent on an annualized basis over the 1970 figure while the median income has gone up only 375 percent. In other words, taxes have gone up nearly twice as fast as incomes. This fact helps explain why American installment debt is now well over $1 trillion, why it now takes two incomes to provide the lifestyle one income provided in the 1960s, the low savings rate, and the stagnant gross national product figures.

Many have concluded that in the face of these seemingly intractable problems, there will be a day of reckoning. The economy has become like a bus rigged with a terrorist bomb. Stop, the terrorist warns, and the bus will be blown to bits. Proceed, and the bus either runs out of gas (in which case it is blown to bits) or ultimately careens out of control. The massive deficits and national debt continue because, if they suddenly ended, the American economy could not withstand the shock. Yet, if they continue, eventually the American economy ends up either in a deflationary bankruptcy or in an inflationary currency meltdown. As Federal Reserve Chairman Alan Greenspan recently stated in congressional testimony: "These trends cannot extend to infinity."

Despite Mr. Greenspan's warning, not a single one of these trends shows even a hint of reversing. To the contrary, they seem to be worsening exponentially like a nuclear chain reaction. Rather than acting on these problems, politicians have changed tactics. They now use disinformation, even propaganda, in an attempt to make it appear as if the problems do not exist. Presidential candidate Ross Perot rightfully likened the situation to a crazy aunt locked in an attic.

Take the government deficit for example. In the 1996 presidential campaign, President Clinton traveled around the country boasting that the budget deficit had been reduced to $106 billion from nearly $200 billion the previous year. That sounded good to most Americans. But President Clinton failed to mention that he accomplished this feat not by reducing spending or through better management (although this is what was implied) but instead by borrowing nearly $160 billion from the Social Security fund. One year before the president's campaign tour, the accumulated national debt stood at $4.983 trillion. As he made his campaign speeches, the debt stood at $5.247 trillion— a difference of $264 billion. Mr. Clinton was off $158 billion in his calculation, demonstrating just how far some inside government are willing to go to keep the facts away from the American people. What's worse, neither the Republicans nor the press questioned the president's figures, an indication if not of complicity then at least of benign neglect. Once again, that crazy aunt in the attic comes to mind. In the real world of international finance, however, these trends have been enough to cause considerable concern.

The International Dollar Crisis

The U.S. dollar is a currency in crisis. It has been steadily debased in fits and starts since World War II. The 1945 dollar is now worth less than 7 cents. The 1971 dollar is now worth 26 cents. The 1980 dollar, during a time when inflation was supposedly "under control," has continued to depreciate and is now worth 55 cents. Against the hard currencies of the world (the Swiss franc, the German mark, and the Japanese yen), the performance of the dollar has been dismal. In 1985 it cost Americans 40 cents to purchase a Swiss franc, 34 cents to purchase a German deutsche mark, and .4 cents to purchase a Japanese yen. In 1994, it cost 73 cents to purchase the franc, 62 cents for the mark, and nearly 1 cent for the yen. In other words, the dollar for all intents and purposes has halved against the world's major currencies. This means all investments would have to appreciate at least as much as the debasement just to keep pace with dollar depriciation. Furthermore, it means we are headed the wrong direction down a one-way street. Someday, the oncoming rush will overwhelm us. Historically, assets denominated in a currency gone bad can be ultimately submerged in a sea of debased paper value, sometimes never to recover again. This is an outcome against which modern investors must protect themselves.

The situation with the U.S. dollar has become so acute that at a recent conference of central bankers in London (December 1995), speakers openly discussed the concept of a tricurrency international monetary system. The yen would dominate Asian trade, the to-be-introduced euro would dominate European trade, and the dollar would dominate trade in the Western hemisphere. Most Americans are unaware that these sorts of discussions are occurring among money men all over the world. Americans are instead led to believe that all is well with their currency and their economy. Central bankers and finance officials talk about how the world got through the fall of the British pound and how "replacing" the dollar could be handled just as judiciously. In other words, the world's central bankers are politely hinting that the dollar is about to be dumped as the world's reserve currency. These ideas are not being debated because confidence in the dollar abounds. To the contrary, those who are in charge of monetary affairs in other countries are deeply concerned about the effect of the debased dollar on their own economies.

We have to assume that it is in the best interest of all nations to let the U.S. dollar down gradually. No one—not the politicians, not the central bankers, not the world's financial centers—wants an international monetary crisis. However, this can be entered under the "best laid plans" column. What the world's financial stalwarts want and what the free market provides might be two different things. For example, it is not difficult to imagine a dollar panic taking shape as

investors the world over scramble to rid themselves of
dollars. After all, there are literally trillions upon trillions of unbacked, fiat dollars circling the globe. Un-
loading unwanted currency is what panics are all
about. These fiat dollars would likely end up on our
doorstep here in the United States, raising the specter
of a hyper-inflationary economy or a massive default
on U.S. Treasury paper. This is the first time in history
that a fiat currency has been used as the world's
reserve currency. No one can accurately guess what
the consequences of its demise might be.

Jürg M. Lattman, a Swiss-based investment coun-
selor, sums up concisely the international view of the
U.S. dollar:

> The U.S. dollar is still the world's reserve currency,
> although its dominance has substantially waned
> since the mid-1970s. The number of countries that
> peg their currencies to the dollar is down by half
> to 24. As a reserve currency, the dollar is sup-
> posed to be a reliable store of value, yet succes-
> sive American governments have failed to fulfill
> this role. Until the early 1980s, America continued
> to boast the largest net foreign assets in the world.
> A decade of massive current account deficits, how-
> ever, has turned America into the world's largest
> debtor. As such, the government may be tempted
> to allow inflation to nibble away at the value of
> the debt and *use devaluation* (emphasis added) to
> reduce its deficits. Hardly desirable properties for
> a reserve currency.

Lest you dismiss the importance of such views,
keep in mind that Lattman is not alone in this senti-
ment. This is precisely how many investment profes-

sionals and economists viewed the Mexican peso in the months and years prior to its precipitous decline in late December 1994. Perhaps it would be wise to listen to and acknowledge the steady drumbeat just before an all-out attack begins. Whether we are about to witness the demise of the U.S. dollar is an open question that will be debated heatedly in the weeks and months to come. Suffice it to say, the symptoms and potential are present for a rapid change in the dollar's advantage as a reserve currency. If that changes, a currency crisis could develop in the United States overnight.

The critical question for investors becomes, how do the financial problems of the U.S. government and the U.S. dollar affect the typical American portfolio? The short answer is, government debt adversely affects the dollar. The value of the dollar, in turn, affects the value of all assets denominated in it. This brings us back full circle to the asset preservation qualities of gold. If you believe these problems could evolve into a currency crisis, then you need to hedge your portfolio with gold and hedge it now.

Gold and the Mexican Peso Debacle: A Lesson in Asset Preservation

An example of how gold protects wealth during a currency crisis can be seen in the December 1994 collapse of the Mexican peso. The now infamous "Christmas surprise" began with an announcement that the government had devalued the peso. Investor reaction was immediate. As soon as the devaluation was announced, long lines formed at the banks and sell orders piled up at brokerage firms, as alarmed investors attempted to get their money out of these institutions before they collapsed. A financial panic lurched into motion. Many were frozen out of the equity markets because they had dropped so precipitously. The peso was in a constant state of deterioration. The inflation rate went to 50 percent immediately and stubbornly stayed at that level. Interest rates soared to 70 percent. Those with credit cards and other interest-sensitive debt, teetered on the brink of bankruptcy simply because they couldn't make the interest payments. In the first year following the devaluation, the price of the peso went from 28.5 cents (U.S.) to 14 cents (U.S.). As I write this chapter, the deterioration continues with the peso at roughly 12 cents. Some predict it is headed for the 10 cent mark.

The gold price, on the other hand, went immediately from roughly 1,200 pesos per ounce to 2,500 pesos per ounce—a mirror image of the peso's fall. Over the course of 1995, gold went over 3,000 pesos—2.5 times its starting point living up to its reputation as the ultimate disaster hedge. (See Figures 2 and 3.) Only a proper diversification before the fall effectively insulated some investors from the currency crisis. This, perhaps, is the most important lesson the Mexican example has to offer. It is one American investors should take to heart. If the protection of your wealth is what you seek, the situation in Mexico shows what gold can do for you as an investor. A 25 percent to 30 percent portfolio diversification into gold would have recouped nearly everything that was lost in the peso and equities markets!

Prior to the devaluation announcement, no warning was given the citizenry by the Mexican govern-

Figure 2. Dollar/ Peso Exchange Rate

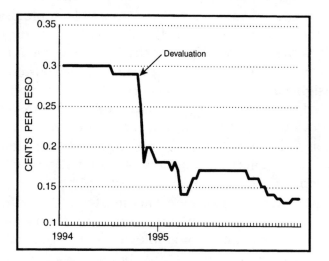

Figure 3. Gold in Pesos Before
and After Mexican Peso Devaluation

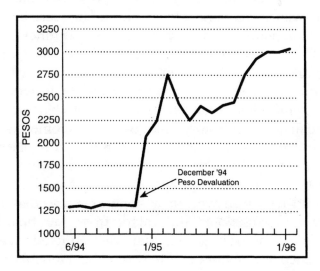

ment or any of the country's major financial institutions. Unfortunately, no financial preparation on the part of the average citizen was possible, unless one had the wisdom to diversify into gold or a currency besides the peso well before the crisis occurred. I use the world *unfortunately* because, if one lacked the foresight to see what direction the economy was headed, one was little more than a sitting duck when the devaluation struck. In the same vein, there is little reason to believe that any strong or rapid deterioration of the U.S. dollar on the international markets will be accompanied by an announcement on the part of the U.S. government. Just as it was in Mexico, the incentive would be to keep any such unraveling under wraps for as long as possible to prevent an all-out currency panic inside our own borders.

Gold, The Ultimate Money and Portfolio Hedge

If an American currency crisis and economic meltdown were to occur, gold would almost certainly behave much as it did in the Mexican currency crisis. Why? Gold is traditionally viewed by people all over the world as the ultimate money, the historically tested and proven method for protecting wealth in even the most trying circumstances. This will not change. It is a peculiarity of history that we have come to this juncture in the evolution of humanity—particularly in the United States with all our modern contrivances— and still believe in the transcendence of gold.

Gold has been with us as long as we have sought civilization, freedom, and safety from the financial, political, and social storms that have afflicted civilization since its beginnings. It saved the French during their disasterous currency inflation of the 1780s. And, it saved Americans during both the continental dollar collapse after the Revolutionary War and the greenback inflation after the Civil War. The twentieth century has been no exception. Gold was a bulwark during the nightmare German inflation that paved the way for Adolf Hitler in the 1920s, the many hyper-inflationary blowoffs in South and Central America, the fall of Saigon, and the collapse of the Soviet Union in the 1990s, not to mention the worldwide Great Depression of the 1930s. These are only a few of the more memorable occasions when gold played a critical role in asset preservation. Many more instances have ended up on the back burner of history.

Gold today continues to play a critical and central role in the financial planning of the world's central banks and that of countless private investors all over the world. The reasons are both simple and practical. Gold affords humanity precisely what it needs from time to time—the protection of wealth against the most threatening circumstances, not the least of which is the destruction of a nation's money by its government. Perhaps something in our ancestral subconscious places this value on gold. Perhaps it is something in our intellectual grasp of history. Whatever the case, gold has always been in the deepest sense a symbol of wealth, freedom, and endurance. Gold is not at all barbarous, as its critics would claim, but instead transcendent. If we own it, we will not only survive but prevail, to borrow the phrase of William Faulkner. "We find comfort in gold. That is why so many of us own it. This is the primary reason for its

allure." In *The New World of Gold*, analyst Timothy
Green sums it up this way:

> What John Maynard Keynes called "the barbarous
> relic" still clings tenaciously to men's hearts. It
> remains the only universally accepted medium of
> exchange, the ultimate currency by which one
> nation, whether capitalist or communist, settles its
> debts with another... The importance governments
> still attach to gold as an essential bastion of a
> nation's wealth is more than equaled by ordinary
> people the world over, who see gold as the sheet
> anchor against devaluations or the hazards of
> war... Even the U.S. government, despite the
> many anti-gold pronouncements over recent years,
> has issued its paratroopers and agents with "es-
> cape and evasion" kits in gold. The Atlantic kit
> includes a gold sovereign, two half sovereigns, a
> Swiss twenty-franc coin, and three gold rings; the
> Southeast Asia kit contains a gold chain, a gold
> pendant, two gold coins, and a gold wristwatch.
> "The gold is for barter purposes," a Pentagon offi-
> cial explains. Actually, a London bullion dealer put
> it best: "Gold is bedrock."

In reality, gold is not an investment at all, as it is
often characterized. Rather, it is a form of money.
Gold does not compete with stocks, bonds and certifi-
cates of deposit because people generally do not purchase gold to make a return on their money. They
purchase it for another reason: to preserve and defend
the wealth they already have. Gold's competitors are
not the IBMs, Intels, and Ford Motor Companies of the
world but instead other forms of money like the U.S.
dollar, the German deutsche mark, the Japanese yen,

the Italian lira, and the British pound. The major difference between the two is that gold is issued by no government or central bank, while national currencies depend entirely upon these institutions for their value. In this sense, gold is more akin to a form of insurance than an investment.

Many economists have published studies on gold. Perhaps Roy Jastrum's *The Golden Constant* is the most famous. They show that gold really does not go up or down at all. Measured in terms of commodities like wheat or corn, its value remains constant over extended periods of time. It is the *paper money* issued by the world's governments and central banks that goes up or down in value.

Gold, it is often said, is the only asset that is not simultaneously someone else's liability. This is a very important concept to grasp. Once you understand this, little else is needed to justify the inclusion of gold in your investment portfolio. When you own a bond, a certified deposit, or an annuity, you have essentially loaned an individual or institution your money. To garner a return *on* that money and the return *of* that money, you are relying upon someone or something's performance. As compensation for that risk, you are paid interest on your money. Of course, stock values are directly related to institutional performance as well. If something goes wrong, the investor is at risk of losing all or part of the investment. Gold, on the other hand, does not pay interest. Therefore, it does not depend on externals for value. If it did, gold owners would be at risk.

Those who criticize gold because it fails to offer a return do not really understand gold's position at the

center as the fixed North Star of asset value around
which all other asset values rotate. Gold is a stand-
alone asset. It relies on no individual or institution for
value.

Gold investors prefer it this way. In the ultimate
sense, this is what money *is* and what money *should
be*. It can always be relied upon when saved or held
as a reserve asset in case of an emergency.

Gold would do for Americans, if necessary, what it
did for the Vietnamese couple I described at the beginning of this chapter, the Mexicans who had the
wisdom to accumulate gold before the peso disaster,
and countless others through the centuries. No matter
what happens in this country with the dollar, with the
debt, with the stock and bond markets, the owner of
gold will find a friend in the yellow metal—something
to rely upon when the chips are down. In gold, investors will find a vehicle to protect their wealth. Gold is
bedrock.

2

B is for...
Bullion Coins: Portable, Liquid, and Beautiful

> *Do not hold as gold all that shines as gold.*
> —*Alain de Lille*

One of the first questions most prospective investors ask is, "What should I buy?" The answer is gold bullion coins like the U.S. Eagle, the Austrian Philharmonic, the South African Krugerrand, and the Canadian Maple Leaf in some combination with pre-1933 U.S. $20 gold pieces. These items should lay the foundation for any sound money portfolio. Jewelry, artistic objects, or very rare, gold collectible coins should not be used for basic asset preservation because their gold value makes up such a small part of their overall value. Gold bullion coins are the safest and best method for protecting wealth and providing insurance against economic calamity. I discuss the reasons for owning the semi-numismatic $20 gold pieces in a later section. (See Chapter 20.) Here I will concentrate on the gold bullion coins.

Shown in this section are the most popular gold bullion coins with their weights, purity, and face values. (See Figure 4.) These coins go up and down with the gold price, are dated with their year of manufacture, and trade at a slight premium over the gold value. They can be bought and sold almost anywhere in the world. They are easily recognizable, of standard weight and purity, and can be easily priced based on their gold content. Many first-time investors believe gold is purchased in the form of the bullion bars depicted in the movies, but in the real world most investors buy 1-ounce bullion coins. This is the most popular, most convenient, and safest way to own gold.

With some exceptions, these coins generally trade at 5 percent to 8 percent over the gold price among most retail firms. This premium above the gold price consists of seigniorage, wholesale markup, and retail markup. Seigniorage is a charge the mint places on the coin to cover manufacturing costs and profits. It usually averages in the 2.5 percent to 3 percent range. Wholesalers add about .5 percent to 1 percent. Retail brokers and dealers usually add commissions from 1 percent to 5 percent, depending on the size of your order and other factors.

Along with the standard 1-ounce coins, most of the mints also manufacture gold coins in smaller denominations of 1/2, 1/4, and 1/10 ounce. Because it costs approximately the same amount of money to manufacture a coin no matter the size, the smaller the coin the greater the premium per ounce. You can find current

Figure 4. Commonly Traded Gold Coins

Austrian Philharmonic
(2000 shillings)
Gross Weight: 31.103 grams (1 troy ounce)
Fineness: .9999 or 24 karats
Diameter: 37 mm
Fine Gold Content: 31.103 grams (1 troy ounce)
Also Available in 1/2, 1/4, 1/10 ounce

American Eagle
$50
Gross Weight: 33.93 grams (1.0910 troy ounces)
Fineness: .916 or 22 karats
Diameter: 32.7 mm
Fine Gold Content: 31.103 grams (1 troy ounce)
Also Available in 1/2, 1/4, 1/10 ounce

Canadian Maple Leaf
$50
Gross Weight: 31.1033 grams (1 troy ounce)
Fineness: .9999 or 24 karats
Diameter: 30 mm
Fine Gold Content: 31.1033 grams (1 troy ounce)
Also Available in 1/2, 1/4, 1/10 ounce

Australian Kangaroo
$100
Gross Weight: 31.1033 grams (1 troy ounce)
Fineness: .9999 or 24 karats
Diameter: 32.10mm
Fine Gold Content: 31.1033 grams (1 troy ounce)

South African Krugerrand
No currency value
Gross Weight: 33.933 grams (1.0909 troy ounces)
Fineness: .916 or 22 karats
Diameter: 34mm
Also Available in 1/2, 1/4, 1/10 ounce

France
20 Francs
Gross Weight: .210 ounce
Fineness: .900 or 21.6 karats
Diameter: 20mm
Fine Gold Content: .1867 ounce

Switzerland
20 Francs
Gross Weight: .210 oounce
Fineness: .900 or 21.6 karats
Diameter: 20mm
Fine Gold Content: .1867 ounce

Great Britain
Sovereign
Gross Weight: .2567 ounce
Fineness: .916
Diameter: 22mm
Fine Gold Content: .2354 ounce

pricing in the financial sections of most local newspapers as well as the national business/financial newspapers. This price is usually the wholesale price which includes seigniorage and wholesale markup but does not include retail markup.

Most experts recommend that investors avoid bullion bars. Although the commission and markups are marginally less on bars than on coins, complications come into play when the time comes to sell bullion. Most dealers will want to see the bars before they buy them because of problems with counterfeiting. Some will not buy without an *assay*, a chemical analysis that determines the gold's purity. Bars present trade and exchange difficulties, unlike bullion coins.

The coining of gold was invented in ancient times as a way to standardize weight and purity and thus to facilitate trade and commerce. History records that Croesus of Lydia was the first to mint pure gold coins. From him the legend of the Midas touch has evolved. Modern gold bullion coins are descendants of the coins first minted by Croesus.

The first *legal tender* bullion coin to gain worldwide use in the modern era was the South African Krugerrand, introduced in 1970. To this day, many gold owners equate gold ownership with Krugerrand ownership. The Krugerrand received its first competition from the Canadian Maple Leaf, introduced in 1979. Eventually the Maple Leaf supplanted the Krugerrand as the world's top seller, gaining a significant market share as a 1-ounce *pure* gold coin. The Krugerrand is .9167 fine. *Fineness* refers to the pure gold weight per 1,000 parts. A fineness of .9167 translates, for example, to 91.67 percent pure gold. Fineness does not refer to the amount of pure gold within the coin but instead to the overall purity. All four coins mentioned here contain 1 pure ounce of gold, though they may weigh more than 1 ounce in total.

Several other countries have introduced competitors in the bullion coin market in recent years. Two are the most notable. The U.S. Eagle, .916 fine, introduced in 1986, has captured a significant share of the world's gold coin market. The Austrian Philharmonic, another pure gold coin, introduced in 1989, has become the best-selling gold bullion coin in the world based on its strong sales in Europe. In 1995 the Austrian Philharmonic led all other bullion coins in international sales at nearly 29 tons, followed by the U.S. Eagle at 18.9 tons, the Canadian Maple Leaf at 10.5 tons, and the Australian Nugget at 10.1 tons. The South African Krugerrand weighed in with 2.3 tons.

Bullion coins present a very stable market for investors. This has been the primary reason for their success. An exception occurred in 1984, when the U.S. Congress banned the import of the Krugerrand as part of the economic sanctions imposed on South Africa. The premium dropped to just slightly above the gold price and never recovered. In 1996, the U.S. Congress authorized the mint to strike pure gold (.9999 fine) U.S. Eagles to compete with the Austrian Philharmonic and Canadian Maple Leaf overseas, particularly in Asia, where pure gold coins are preferred.

In the case of bullion bars, most dealers will not lock in a price until they have received the merchandise and have had a chance to examine it. With bullion coins, if you have a good relationship with your dealer or broker, you can lock in a price over the phone because the buyer has confidence in what will be received. Bullion bars could also present problems for those wishing to trade gold for merchandise in the event of an economic breakdown because the individual receiving the gold bullion has no way of knowing whether it's counterfeit. It is best to stick with the coins that are difficult to counterfeit. The marginal added cost on bullion coins is a small price to pay when weighed against the potential disadvantages of owning bars.

Gold bullion coins are priced in the United States using COMEX in New York as price basis. The price changes constantly during the trading day. Some dealers will allow their better customers to lock in prices over the telephone, but this usually requires that you have already established some kind of relationship with the dealer or broker. In lieu of locking in over the telephone, your dealer may require that good funds be on hand—by wire or cashiers' check—before your purchase price is set. Upon receiving your funds, dealers will either execute your order at market or contact you before locking in the price, depending upon your wishes. Differences between the amount you send and your actual price are then paid by check before actual delivery. Bullion coins are available at banks, brokerage firms, gold bullion firms, and coin dealers. Banks have largely withdrawn from this market in the United States, having found it difficult to make the two-way market investors require. A few of the large Wall Street banks do still offer this service. Brokerage firms have never been major players in the gold bullion coin market. In most cases, they have found it difficult to compete price-wise with those who specialize in gold.

As I will point out in Chapter 3, when choosing a gold firm it is extremely important for investors to develop a relationship with one that specializes in precious metals and has a history of trading in this market. Although the issues are covered in some detail in that chapter, suffice it to say here that it is to the investor's advantage to find someone knowledgeable, experienced, and reputable in this highly specialized field. Choosing the right gold connection is crucial. The right firm can give you solid guidance in your portfolio decisions, including which bullion coins best fit your particular strategy and economic viewpoint. The best decisions on gold are made under the guidance of an expert who can appreciate and understand your needs.

3

C is for...
Choosing a Gold Firm

W ho you do business with is one of the most important aspects of gold investing. The gold business, like almost all other areas of the investment business, has had problems with scoundrels—boiler room operators, scam operations, fly-by-night firms, and the like. The dissemination of poor, self-serving advice from these type of firms—not to mention potential fraudulent activity—is a problem to which all potential gold investors should be alert. These are unfortunate situations, but it needs to be said that it is the unscrupulous few who impose a heavy burden on the honest and reputable many. To make a long story short, it pays to be cautious while creating a comfort zone in which you can make your gold purchases with a strong degree of safety.

Gold requires an element of trust not present in other financial transactions. Even though stock and bond investors must part with their money before they receive what they have purchased, most people have become accustomed to this arrangement. Most do not even take delivery of stocks or bonds but simply leave them in their accounts at stock brokerage firms or in mutual funds. Most gold investors, on the other hand, want immediate possession of their metal. Since most people psychologically perceive gold higher on the value scale than other things, an ancient genetic warning somewhere in the mind flashes "caution, caution, caution." Since no gold dealer in the world will send metal without receiving "good funds" first, trust becomes the critical element to completing the transaction. Who you deal with becomes critically important from your point of view. Since you have to buy from someone, the best and only method is to develop some strong criteria and to then find a firm that measures up to your standards. Here are a few rules that will help raise your comfort level:

1. Deal only with firms that have been around a long time. Five years is good, ten years or more is even better. As gold begins to rise, new firms will begin to pop up like the flowers in spring. Some will be solid, most will not. Firms ten years old or more have been around through thick and thin. They are dedicated to the gold market and are usually owned by individuals who are true believers. These are the best firms with which to establish a relationship.

2. Check for credentials. What are the professional organizations to which the firm belongs? Request written information about the firm. Do not buy until you have reviewed it and checked out the firm. Most of the better firms have an introductory packet you can request. In it is much of the information you will need to begin your due diligence. Better business bureaus have gone to automated inquiry programs in most areas, which makes it easy to check out a firm. If the organization is not a member of the local better business bureau, this should serve as a warning. If a company has had complaints, it might be worthwhile to check with the bureau as to how those complaints were handled. The existence of a complaint is not proof that you are in contact with a questionable firm. However, if the complaints have not been properly handled, there is cause for concern.

Most of the top gold dealers belong to the Industry Council for Tangible Assets (ICTA). Although ICTA does not rate gold firms or in any way regulate them, it is good for you as a consumer to know how long the firm you are considering has been a member. It will confirm their claims of longevity. Another option is to contact your state attorney general's office and ask if they have had any complaints on the company. Most AGs know which firms have had problems. Although they cannot come right out and say whether the company is a good or bad one, they might mention that there have been unresolved complaints.

3. Ask detailed questions about how transactions are going to take place. When is the price set? How long for delivery? Bullion and bullion coins should come to you within ten business days. Semi-numismatic (semi-rare coin or pre-1933 U.S. gold coin) and numismatic (rare coin) transactions may take longer. Make sure delivery times are within these industry standards. If they are not, it is a red flag.

4. If you receive information from a good firm, and you like what you see and hear, go with them. If you have the slightest doubt, especially if the firm does not sufficiently meet the criteria above, then go back to square one and start over. Better to be safe than sorry.

5. Beware of sales pitches. If the firm calls you repeatedly, badgers you, or calls with one "great deal" after another, be careful. There might be something wrong. If they persist in trying to sell you something in which you have no interest, this is another red flag. Resist and seek more information and other opinions. Do not make a decision until you have received sufficient information.

6. Check and compare pricing. Cheaper is not always better. In fact, below-market pricing should flash a warning light. If a deal sounds too good to be true, it probably is.

7. Trust referrals. The best firm to deal with is the one you are referred to by a trusted friend or family member who has had experience with that firm. Such experience is invaluable.

Choosing the right gold firm has other advantages. First, a firm that has been around awhile obviously has had experience dealing in the gold market. It can therefore guide you over some of the hurdles. It can also answer your questions quickly and thoroughly. The chances of receiving the correct information are greatly heightened. For most investors, "What to buy?" at some point becomes an important question. A good gold broker can put you on the right path after asking just a few questions like, "Why are you buying gold?" or, "What are you thinking about these days to prompt your looking into gold?" The broker who doesn't ask such questions is probably inexperienced and is touting what the firm wants him to tout. An interest in you specifically as an investor is an indicator that you might have found a firm worth checking into further.

Second, it is extremely important for most investors to find a firm with which they have a philosophical affinity. A shared viewpoint on economic and political circumstances is a clue that this firm can meet your needs both now and in the future as circumstances change.

Third, a *client-oriented* company that takes an interest in your gold investment is far preferable to a *customer-oriented* company. Customer-oriented companies compete primarily on price with little regard to the overall needs of the client. These companies are usually staffed by low-paid employees who essentially serve a clerking function. A question like "Why are you buying gold?" would never be asked because the objective is to fill the order and move on to the next transaction. You say you want gold coin X. They may sell you gold coin X with little regard to the reasons why you are buying gold or the fact that the coin might not be the best coin for you based on your objectives. Client-based firms are more interested in you as an individual. A good gold broker will ask a few key questions to get a "feel" for the client. If that occurs, you know you are on the right track.

Last but not least, choosing the right firm is essential to properly managing the long-term nature of your gold holdings. During your time as a gold owner, much is likely to change in this country. You will want to stay informed. The better gold firms usually offer information services like newsletters, market reports, and the like. In addition, brokers at these firms usually make themselves available for further consultation even after you have made your purchase. They spend a great deal of time keeping themselves informed. Your firm will be an important resource for you as the years go by. You will also want to form a relationship with a firm that will be around for additional purchases and future sales. In short, spend some time choosing a gold firm. Your future as a gold investor depends upon choosing a good one.

4

D is for...

Diversification: Now More Than Ever

Chairman of the U.S. Federal Reserve Alan Greenspan is not one given to dramatic statements about gold, or anything else for that matter. Nevertheless, he made the following out-of-character comment at a recent Congressional hearing:

> I do think there is a considerable amount of information about the nature of a domestic currency from observing its price in terms of gold. It is a longer-term issue. It is an issue which I think is relevant, and if you don't believe that, you always have to ask the question why it is that central banks hold so much gold which earns no interest and which costs them money to store. The answer is obvious: they consider it of significant value, and, indeed, they consider it the ultimate means of payment, one which does not require any form of endorsement. There is something out there that is terribly important that the gold price is telling us.

I think that disregarding it is to fail to recognize
certain crucial aspects of the value of currencies.

This brief but revealing statement from a man who
spends a good part of his day worrying about currency values illustrates the importance of gold in portfolio diversification, not just for central banks but for
private investors as well. As a matter of fact, if you
were to ask a hundred gold buyers why they own
gold, a respectable majority would immediately answer, "For diversification." Most investors equate diversification with peace of mind. Diversification im-
plies preparation for a variety of potential economic
events. If the portfolio is properly structured, it matters
not if stock markets crash, or bonds lose value, or
currencies suffer debasement. The hard assets of the
portfolio will pick up the slack.

Swiss money managers, renowned for their ability
to handle money and investments of some of the
world's wealthiest people, traditionally recommend a
diversification into gold of 15 percent to 25 percent for
good reason. Beyond the normal risks of market fluc-
tuations associated with stock and bond investments,
there is the additional danger of depreciation in the
currency underlying the stock or bond. Denominated
in a domestic currency (pesos, yen, marks, dollars),
these investments rely on sound central bank and
government currency management policies to maintain
their value. It is conceivable that a corporation or
municipality, for example, could be perfectly man-
aged, yet its bonds could still erode in value due to
politically expedient currency debasement on the part
of federal authorities. The 1994 peso devaluation in
Mexico is a prime example of this potential problem.

On the other hand, the Swiss take their own advice. The Swiss franc is backed at a very high percentage with gold, and their gold reserves have not been reduced an ounce in more than twenty years. As a result, the Swiss franc has been one of the most solid, reliable, and desirable currencies in the world for decades.

Gold diversification makes particularly good sense when stock and bond markets have reached cyclical highs—even if the plateau extends over a period of months or years. In many cases (but not always), gold moves opposite the trend in equities markets. In 1997 when the U.S. stock market was at an all-time high, many investors began to move out of stocks and bonds and into gold with the hope of securing profits garnered in those markets. This trend is likely to continue in future years no matter how the stock market performs simply because such a strategy amounts to common-sense portfolio management. Even if gold were to remain the same as equities corrected, the investor will have preserved the profits previously gained in equities by switching to gold. This is a strategy many investors undertook in the mid-1970s as the stock market appeared to be topping, which it was. Investors were richly rewarded. The Dow Jones corrected nearly 40 percent while gold went from roughly $60 per ounce to nearly $200 per ounce in the same period. From there the stock market languished while gold continued it historic climb to nearly $900 per ounce.

The Gold Institute released a study several years ago on the purchasing power of currencies in various countries from 1965 to 1985. Though dated, the study suggests a trend that calls into question the viability of many national currencies as a store of value. In Germany the mark decreased roughly 60 percent over the period, and it is usually viewed as a "hard" currency. The U.S. dollar decreased 70 percent. The Canadian dollar fell 80 percent. The Mexican peso dropped 95 percent, and that was before the 1994 devaluation! In other words, there are few paper currencies that serve adequately as a store of value. There are plenty of reasons for diversifying with gold no matter what country you call home.

As I pointed out in Chapter 1, gold as an asset in your portfolio has a single great attribute: it is not simultaneously someone else's liability. It is the primary asset of last resort, meaning that its long-term value does not depend on the performance of another individual or institution. This is what Mr. Greenspan is referring to when he says gold does not require "endorsement." As it does for the world's central banks, a solid diversification into gold makes sense for the average investor. Between 15 percent and 25 percent of one's assets should be devoted to gold ownership as a prudent hedge in one's overall investment portfolio.

5

E is for...
Education: The Key to Successful Gold Investing

> *Truth must be ground for every man by himself out of its husk, with such help as he can get, indeed, but not without stern labor of his own.*
> —*John Ruskin*

Most investment professionals tell you, "Buy the book before you buy the investment." In the case of gold, since the selection of books on the subject matter is limited, a more proper axiom might be, "Buy the newsletter(s) before you buy the investment." Most of the "best" information on gold—factual, analytical, and opinion—is more readily available in monthly newsletters than at your local bookstore. Newsletters are also the best source for "how to" information on gold. This is not to say there are not a few good books and magazine articles available on the subject of gold that you should check out. Check with your local bookstores and libraries or watch for advertisements in the financial newspapers, magazines, or on radio and television. No matter how you obtain your education, it is critical for you to have solid knowledge about gold before making your first purchase.

This book will provide the necessary introductory information. A few good newsletters can play *the* critical role of keeping you informed on an ongoing basis. Some of the best analytical work today is not being done at the university level or even in the research departments of the various large Wall Street firms but instead in the fast growing area of independent newsletter publishing. The widespread availability of information and research data through computerization has created a whole new intellectual community no longer tied to university libraries or corporate databases. The modern newsletter writer equipped with a personal computer and access to vast information resources is not restrained institutionally. They quite often produce not only interesting but also enormously useful work for "seekers of the truth." Keep in mind that these newsletters offer the personal views and understandings of the writers. Sometimes they are right, sometimes they are wrong. Their views are quite often controversial and at times off the beaten path. You are the final arbiter and decision maker. Read carefully, analyze, and form your own opinions.

A listing of newsletters that deals with gold and related issues appears in Appendix 1. The newsletters are listed alphabetically, not by preference. A short review is included so that you have some idea what you're buying before you buy it. Many newsletters offer three- and six-month trial subscriptions. Take advantage of trial subscriptions. This way, you can see which particular newsletters best suit your purposes. Any list, like that in Appendix 1, is partial out of necessity. Most of those listed have a strong connection to gold or a sound understanding of the economic and political issues surrounding the gold market.

You can get good (although sanitized) day-to-day information through your local newspaper, financial publications, and TV news—particularly the business television channels where information on gold appears regularly. Many think it is fair to say that the traditional press, with a few exceptions, has a strong anti-gold bias. This must be taken into account. Another good source of general information and opinion is talk radio. Talk radio may be one of the last bastions of free thought in America. No matter what your political persuasion, these shows can be a good source of information, much of which you are unlikely to find in the traditional media.

The challenge of the rest of the 1990s and the beginning of the twenty-first century will be to find, segregate, absorb, and utilize large amounts of information. With respect to investments, the information you get and your own analytical abilities will be the difference between success and failure. This holds true not only for your rationale but also for your choices and timing strategies. Newsletters will continue to be a necessary resource outside of traditional sources of news and opinion. With respect to gold and the political and economic opinions that revolve around it, newsletters could turn out to be the vital sources of independent information and opinion you will not want to be without.

6

F is for...
Fundamentals: Supply and Demand

Supply/demand tables (Figure 5) are the type of dry economic statistics that people usually try to avoid like the latest flu virus. But before you fast-forward through this section, keep in mind that most experts believe this unusually strong, fundamental picture will be the engine that drives the next bull market in gold. If asset preservation (wealth protection) provides the basic motivation for gold ownership, then profit potential could be an attractive sidebar to gold's story as we approach the twenty-first century. That potential relies on the supply/demand fundamentals. To be sure, understanding this relationship—between how much is produced and how much is consumed—will be *the* key to making you a *competent* and *confident* gold investor. Many gold analysts believe gold will exceed its old high of $875 per ounce sometime in the 1990s, not because of an economic crisis but simply because mine production will fall considerably short of demand.

Figure 5. Western World Gold Supply and Demand 1986-1995

	1986	1987	1988	1989	1990	1991	1992	1993	1994	1995
Supply										
Mine production	1296	1384	1551	1683	1755	1790	1872	1904	1897	1890
Former communist bloc	402	303	263	266	392	230	63	178	109	102
Net official sales				366	13	25	624	446	80	232
Old gold scrap	513	454	375	372	510	450	448	532	572	583
Gold loans	17	55	164	78	5					
Forward sales	20	72	126	116	222	96	156	217	163	461
Option hedging	8	22	83		7	15	103		57	87
Implied disinvestments			160	20		290			181	
Total Supply	**2255**	**2290**	**2722**	**2901**	**2904**	**2896**	**3266**	**3277**	**3060**	**3355**
Demand										
Jewelery	1224	1270	1579	1960	2099	2176	2519	2342	2377	2537
Electronics	125	126	135	139	148	152	143	155	168	185
Other	471	330	283	274	261	289	257	291	261	285
Total fabrications	1819	1725	1976	2373	2508	2617	2919	2788	2806	3008
Net official purchases	145	72	285							
Bar hoarding	214	259	461	514	203	233	243	122	203	281
Gold loans						45	85	65	52	23
Option hedging								31		
Implied investments	78	233		15	13		19	271		44
Total demand	**2255**	**2290**	**2272**	**2901**	**2904**	**2896**	**3266**	**3277**	**3060**	**3355**
London gold price	367.92	446.07	436.77	380.79	383.59	362.26	343.95	359.82	384.15	384.05

Statistics courtesy of Gold Fields Mineral Services, London, England, Gold 1996

The fundamental picture is bullish indeed. In 1971, the United States severed the link between the dollar and gold and ushered in the era of the unbacked fiat dollar. (See Chapter 8.) Then the total annual world demand hovered around 1,300 tons. Now the annual demand for gold in Asia itself is over 1,000 tons. Some gold market experts estimate that sometime early in the twenty-first century the demand for gold in mainland China alone will reach 1,000 tons. That is just in one country in the populous, increasingly prosperous Pacific Rim. Already the gap between mine production (1,890 tons) and fabrication uses (3,008 tons) is 1,118 tons—a shortfall of nearly 37 percent made up by above-ground sources. (See Figure 6.) Since there are

**Figure 6. Gold Fabrication and Mine Production
Worldwide 1986 to 1995**

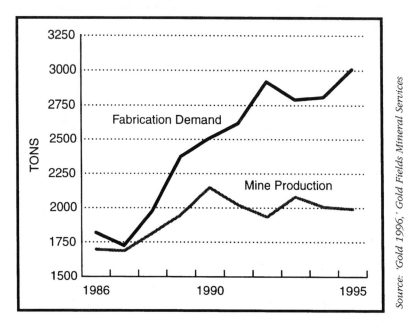

Source: 'Gold 1996,' Gold Fields Mineral Services

limits to the amount of gold these above ground sources (primarily the world's central banks) can supply, the question becomes: what happens to the price once these sources stop supplying the market? When you take into account the forecast growth in gold demand in Asia along with the burgeoning growth in demand in other areas of the globe, in the absence of a major currency crisis, it is not difficult to see how some experts justify their positive forecasts for gold. The following is a short, but comprehensive, view of the supply/demand situation.

Supply

The total supply of gold as shown in the accompanying table is 3,355 tons, and 1,890 of those tons come from the world's gold mines. Other sources of supply, such as scrap, mine company forward selling (actually supplied by the central banks), and official government and (Figure 5. Western World Gold Supply and Demand 1986-1995) central bank sales play an important role in the overall picture. But the mines are the primary source, supplying roughly 60 percent of the gold used annually.

Let's concentrate first on the gold mines since they are the primary factor on the supply side. The mines will play a significant role in the gold market now and in the future, both as outright producers and as forward sellers.

Mine Production

South Africa reigns as the world's greatest producer of gold (roughly 27 percent of the total) and has been since most people can remember. The United States

(17 percent) is second, a position it inherited from the old Soviet Union in 1990 mostly by default. Australia (13 percent) is third, while Canada (8 percent) displaced Russia (7.5 percent) in 1996 for fourth. South Africa has been the dominant gold producer for years, but its production has been in continuous and rapid decline. For years, labor problems both before and during the Mandela years have put a damper on production. These problems seem to be worsening. A concomitant problem has been the very deep mines themselves, which increase mining costs and reduce production. In 1985 South African production was 672 tons. By 1995 it had plummeted to 522 tons, down 22 percent. Except for some intermittent years of marginal improvement, the trend has been decidedly downward. There are projections that U.S. production will overtake South Africa's in the next decade, but such an outcome remains to be seen because of the stiff environmental laws in this country. A report from Gold Fields Mineral Services (GFMS), *Gold 1996*, says this about the current situation in South Africa:

> Gold production in South Africa dropped by over 10 percent in 1995... This dramatic decline, the largest both in percentage and absolute terms since the early 1970s, took the country's output to the lowest level in 40 years.

In short, the South African mines have nearly played out. South African mining companies have begun aggressive programs to find new sources of gold outside South Africa's borders.

Russia, once the second largest gold producer in the world, has suffered labor and production problems of its own and has slipped to number five. The most recent fundamentals tables list the production of the various republics of the old Soviet Union as separate producers. The old tables combine them under one heading, the Soviet Union. Even when you add back the production of Uzbekistan (which, along with Russia, accounts for over 90 percent of the old Soviet Union's production), the supply from the old Soviet Union has dropped considerably. The situations in South Africa and the old Soviet Union are not likely to improve anytime soon. If there is to be an increase in gold production internationally, it will have to come from somewhere else. Much speculation has appeared in recent years as to what would happen if the mining industry should begin breaking down in these two countries due to social and political pressures. It is not difficult to guess the consequences if one-third of international production begins to disappear from the supply/demand tables.

The United States is the second largest gold producer, principally through the default of the old Soviet Union. The strong increase (from 118.3 tons to 326 tons) in production since 1986 is of more than passing interest to gold investors, if for no other reason than to try to assess whether this growth has peaked. In 1994, U.S. gold production declined for the first time in ten years. The GFMS 1995 survey reports:

> If Barrick Gold's Goldstrike Mine (America's largest gold mine), where the considerable expansion in gold production over the past few years has all but ended, is excluded from the calculation, then the country's output would have actually fallen in 1993 and 1994.

Overall, mining in the United States is problematic. Environmental and permitting restrictions continue to beset the expansion of the industry. Many mining companies are concentrating their exploration capital in more hospitable environs outside the United States. The multi-billion-dollar environmental disaster at the Summitville mine in Colorado, from which cyanide tailings continue to leach unabated into the Arkansas River, has put a damper on further exploration within the borders of the United States.

Most of the action in mining stocks these days has to do with exploration and production possibilities in Latin and South America and Africa. China, now the sixth largest gold producer, also presents some interesting possibilities. Production in these countries, however, is small in the overall context and is not likely to have a major impact on the supply/demand tables until well into the twenty-first century.

Overall mine production has leveled at 1800 - 1900 ton mark while usage is still growing, up almost 10 percent in 1995. Production growth, as pointed out earlier, has been unable to keep pace with the growth in demand. Since 1986 mine production has increased 46 percent while fabrication has grown by 65 percent.

Mine Companies Forward Selling

The mining companies impact the gold market not just by the amount of gold they produce annually but also by the amount they sell forward for future delivery as part of their mine production financing programs. This activity, often referred to as *hedging*, or *forward selling,* is not as complicated as it sounds. But its implications for the marketplace are complicated indeed. In 1995, mine company forward selling accounted for 461 tons of the supply, or nearly 14 percent. Remove that supply from the tables and you have a runaway gold price. This aspect of the supply table is very important for investors to understand.

The two principal players in forward selling are the mines and the central banks. For the mines, forward selling is a convenient and inexpensive form of financing. For the central banks, it is a means to make interest on an otherwise dormant balance sheet item. Ian Cox, who formerly headed the trading desk at London's Samuel Montagu, the longtime British gold dealer, writes:

> By mid-1993 it is estimated that 2,000 tons [of gold] were on loan in the market, almost the equivalent of one year's output of the world's gold mines... European central banks lend about 600 tons, 40 percent of the total supplied, but central banks from other parts of the world, notably Latin America and East Asia, have also begun to mobilize a portion of their gold holdings in this way....

The central banks actually take gold out of their holdings and loan it to the mines at interest rates that ranged in 1995 from .5 percent to 6 percent. Private gold bullion banks like Morgan Stanley and Republic National in New York act as intermediaries, or brokers to these transactions. The mines then sell the gold on the open market through the bullion banks to raise capital for their mining operations through the bullion banks. This obviously has a depressing effect on the price. As more and more pressure mounts on the existing gold reserves at the central banks, the lease

rate rises. Whenever it reaches the domestic currency
lending rate, the incentive is to curtail borrowing gold
and instead borrow the currency, or curtail borrowing
entirely.

In 1996, stockholders in the mining companies began to question these forward selling policies. If a
mining company has sold most of its production forward and the price explodes to the upside, the mining
company's profits suffer because their metal will have
already been sold at substantially less. As a result,
stock prices suffer, putting the stockholders at odds
with the managers. The question arises, why would a
mining company be interested in this sort of financing
in the first place? The answer is, it is cheap financing
as long as the price doesn't rise. Once the price begins
rising, however, forward selling loses its appeal because it essentially sells gold short. In a rising market,
the mines would be forced to repay the gold to the
central banks at what could be an astronomical price.
With the threat of inflation on the rise internationally,
this scenario could become a reality the mining companies will not relish. The once cozy, symbiotic relationship between the mines and the central banks
could turn nasty.

We got a glimpse of what could happen in Janu-
ary 1996, when gold pushed over the $400 market
price for the first time since 1987. The move was
accompanied by rumors that Barrick Gold was about
to abandon its policy of selling gold forward, a move
sure to be followed by other industry leaders since
Barrick had been the largest-volume forward seller for
some time. The price quickly spurted to the $420
level. As it turned out, Barrick officially announced it

was reducing its forward positions by a third rather than abandoning the policy entirely, but the psychological impact on the market was as if they had abandoned it entirely. Why was this so important to the gold market?

The answer lies in a close examination of the supply/demand tables. Forward sales, which played only a minor role in the gold supply in 1985 (less than 1 percent of the total), began to play a major role in the market in 1990 (about 7.5 percent) and from that point forward. In 1995 forward sales by mining companies amounted to 461 tons—an almost 250 percent increase over 1994 and representing nearly 14 percent of the supply! Many analysts believe forward sales by mining companies became the major restraint on the gold price for most of the early 1990s, especially in 1995, when worldwide demand exploded.

In one recent case, a mining company in South Africa, Johannesburg Consolidated, sold 7.3 million ounces of gold forward—seven years of production for that company and the equivalent of Australia's production for an entire year! This is gold in the ground, not yet mined, gold sold by a company that operates in a country with serious political and social problems. This type of sale raises a number of interesting questions. What happens if the social situation in South Africa explodes? This is a scenario not beyond rational expectations. In lieu of that, what happens to Johannesburg Consolidated if the price moves substantially higher? What happens when it has to cover? Johannesburg Consolidated will have to go into the market to balance the equation as *buyers,* with the

result of putting extraordinary pressure on the already
thin gold supply.

In addition to the problems at the mines with respect to forward selling, Montagu's Ian Cox sees difficulties with the central banks continuing to provide
gold liquidity:

> The question has been asked whether the central
> banks should continue to lend to the market,
> when it would appear that one of the direct con-
> sequences is to facilitate mine hedge selling,
> which in turn has an impact on the gold price, and
> hence the value of official reserves.

Beyond that consideration is whether the central
banks involved in this activity have reached their limits with respect to the prudent management of gold
reserves.

All in all, we are coming to a place where forward
selling may disappear from the supply/demand tables
or at least suffer severe reductions, adding more evidence to the bullish case for gold.

Central Bank Selling

Net official sales of gold plummeted from 622 tons
in 1992 and 445 tons in 1993 to 232 tons in 1995.
Since 1968, central bank gold reserves in the industrial
countries have dropped nearly 30 percent. Much of
the gold selling by central banks in recent years has
been the result of European selling to meet the requirements of the new European Monetary Union as
mandated by the Maastricht Treaty. Belgium was particularly active in 1995, delivering to the market almost
half the gross sales picked up in the GFMS study.

Belgium announced that most of this gold was sold to another unnamed central bank. Japan has been proffered by many analysts as the likely buyer. With respect to the long-term effect of official sector sales, it should be understood by gold investors that central bank selling has been a constant on the supply side for decades and will likely continue to be for the foreseeable future. The market tends to absorb the gold with little difficulty and, although there is usually short-term pressure on the price, the long-term effects of central bank sales are negligible. Insofar as producer hedging has offered the central banks an alternative to outright selling, these sales have been limited to quasilegal operations such as Belgium's sale in 1995 and that of the Netherlands in 1994.

The Combined Effects of Forward Selling, Net Official Sales, and Option Hedging

When you combine official sales with forward selling and option hedging—all central bank operations— an interesting picture emerges. There is an inverse relationship between these combined sales and the gold price. (See Figure 7.) When the intervention (for lack of a better word) is in progress, the price is restrained. When the intervention is abandoned, the price begins rising more quickly than it would under normal circumstances because of built-up price pressure. This explains the spikes that characterize and dominate the gold charts. Had the official sector not been a seller/lender, the rise in price would have been gradual and less dramatic. There possibly even would have been less of a runup.

Figure 7. Combined Central Bank Official Sales, Loans, Option Hedging, and the Gold Price

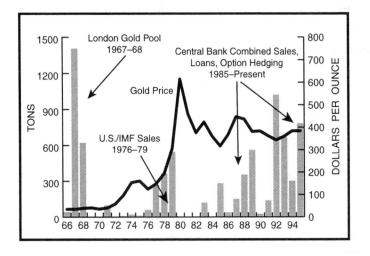

This inverse relationship between central bank gold sales and loans and the gold price is evident in the chart. In the 1960s, through the London Gold Pool (with the United States as the central player) and again in the mid-1970s, through the International Monetary Fund/U.S. Treasury sales, the United States made massive interventions in the gold market to keep the price from reflecting dollar weakness. In the late 1960s, the the U.S. government mandated price was $35 per ounce. Once the intervention was lifted in 1974 the market rose to nearly $200 per ounce. In the mid-1970s the target price was $150 per ounce, and the U.S./IMF did succeed temporarily in driving the price to $100 per ounce. From there demand became unstoppable as the inflation rate rose and the dollar nose-dived. The peak in 1980 was $875—almost nine times the starting point.

In those early instances of intervention in the gold market, the primary interest of interventionists was to hold down gold so that U.S. policies with respect to the dollar would not become suspect. Dollar inflation was bubbling just beneath the surface. Monetary and government officials acted to keep the price of gold down so that the dollar would not come under further attack. Once the intervention was abandoned, gold found its natural price level. As the graph shows, however, these policies have never kept gold from achieving its desired level vis-à-vis the dollar. They have simply been delaying actions just prior to a full retreat. Essentially, the war was lost before it was even fought.

Now the central banks, knowingly or not, are engaged in a new battle in the war against gold. Since 1989 the central banks in combined sales and forward sales have put nearly 3,000 tons of gold on the market. The net effect has been to keep the price of gold around $400 per ounce.

The unintended consequences has been that central bank lending and sales have been fairly good indicators of upcoming gold spikes. Time will tell whether the current intervention has run its course. But the evidence from the past is clear: when central bank intervention is removed from the market, a spike occurs. GFMS reports that in the second half of 1995 central banks became net buyers of gold. This could be an indicator of things to come.

Demand

On the other side of the gold equation, jewelry accounts for over 75 percent of the annual gold demand. A large portion is usually designated as investment jewelry, primarily in Asia. The remainder of demand comes from investment, electronic uses, and a myriad of other, smaller usage categories. The real story on the demand side of the equation is not so much what gold is used for but where it's going. This presages positive trends for gold that are likely to buttress the market for years to come.

The growth in Asia—India, Japan, China, and Taiwan—has been dramatic. (See Figure 8.) The Pacific Rim in general is the fastest-growing economic area in the world, and gold demand is growing with it. The World Gold Council reports growth in those countries is for distinctly different reasons:

> Gold demand set a record in 1995, with the markets monitored by the World Gold Council rising to 2,746 tonnes, 7.6 percent above 1992, the previous peak year. A number of gold's qualities manifested themselves convincingly: its indestructibility and security in times of financial uncertainty triggered a 63 percent jump, to 160 tonnes, in Japanese investment demand; its role as a hedge against currency depreciation contributed to the strength of demand in India and Turkey; its cultural and religious significance continued to underpin demand growth in several Middle Eastern and Asian markets... 1995 turned out to be a banner off-take year for developed and developing countries.

In India, the largest gold consumer in the world and a culture where gold plays a significant role, new found prosperity is pushing gold demand to record levels—up 14 percent in 1995 alone. The Japanese are buying gold for investment purposes (up 63 percent in 1995) due to a heightening bank crisis and the yen continuing to provide strong international purchasing power. That makes gold a bargain. In addition, the Japanese central bank has become a gold buyer, adding 2.1 million ounces to its reserves in 1995. China has also become a stronger player in the gold market in recent years. Europe has also shown growth, with demand up over 60 percent since 1986. The prospects for further growth in Europe are strong, as European citizens react to various currency and political changes

Figure 8. Asian Gold Demand 1986 to Present

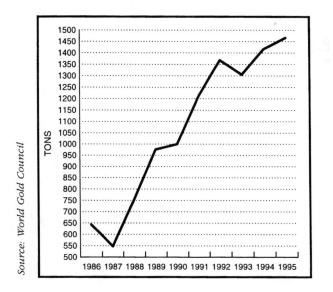

having to do with European unification under the Brussels-based European Union. U.S. demand has grown as well—up 27 percent since 1986.

In 1995, gold bar hoarding worldwide increased by 43 percent, a reflection of growing apprehension in the international investment community. In the future some of the fastest-growing investment markets will most likely be Japan, the United States, and Western Europe, once again reflecting growing apprehension about economic and financial uncertainty in these countries.

In general, worldwide demand has doubled over the last decade. Demand in 1995 increased by 7 percent in a year of relatively stable currency markets to a record 3,257 tons. There is little on the horizon to prevent this growth trend from extending into the twenty-first century. As a matter of fact, these trends would likely accelerate if accompanied by currency problems, particularly with the dollar.

Conclusion

Now you have a basic understanding of what makes the gold market tick. This is in no way meant to be a comprehensive analysis of the supply/demand fundamentals of gold. Whole volumes have been devoted to this type of analysis. My purpose has been to provide an introduction to the basic principles. If you would like a deeper understanding, Gold Fields Mineral Services of London, England, offers perhaps the best in-depth analysis available. Their address is included in Appendix 1 as part of the newsletter review.

The most intriguing aspect of the supply/demand fundamentals is that gold appears to offer an opportunity at a time when further problems for the dollar seem to looming on the horizon. (See Chapter 7 on government debt.) The fundamental picture for gold— accelerating demand and decelerating mine production combined with the possibility of curtailed central bank involvement on the supply side—presents an opportunity unlike anything that has occurred in the gold market since the United States abandoned its interventionist gold policies in the 1970s. You will want to keep yourself apprised of this situation as it evolves in the coming years. In the meantime, it appears gold is presenting an interesting opportunity.

7

G is for...
Government Debt: Are We Going the Way of Mexico?

> The imitations of gold and silver will become inflated
> which after the rape are thrown into the fire,
> After discovering all is exhausted and dissipated by debt.
> All scripts and bonds are wiped out.
> —Michel de Nostradamus, *The Centuries*, 1555

Perhaps Nostradamus was talking about the Mexico of December 1994 when he penned the famous quatrain above, perhaps the United States in the not-too-distant future. Whatever the case, Nostradamus could not have known about paper money because it did not exist in sixteenth-century Europe. This adds an interesting twist to the quatrain. The money was in fact gold and silver coin.

This malediction—one of several that has materialized as predicted by the controversial seer—could apply to any number of currency panics that have occurred in Western civilization since the time of Nostradamus. But for those with an understanding of the current economic situation in the United States, it has more than a foreboding ring of truth. Whether you believe the prognostications of Nostradamus or rely on the analysis of more earthbound economic observers, this quatrain is certainly food for thought.

The national debt—now over $5 trillion and growing exponentially—lies at the heart of what ails this country. (See Figure 9.) Your understanding of the problem and how it affects your financial portfolio will be critical to your financial well-being in the years to come.

The recent Mexican devaluation, as I pointed in Chapter 1, illustrates what could be expected if the debt problem were to get out of control in the United States. The United States is following closely along the same profligate path of Mexico. Debt monetization, the abnormal increase in foreign-held debt, currency inflation—all characterize the U.S. economy today just

Figure 9. Accumulated Federal Debt 1972 to 1995

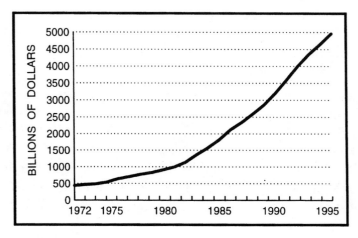

Data source: The Statistical Abstract of the United States, 1995, U.S. Department of Commerce

as they did Mexico's economy before the devaluation. What has saved this country thus far from Mexico's fate is the advantage of the dollar as the world's chief reserve currency. Take away the reserve currency advantage, and the United States could very well have already tumbled into the hyperinflationary abyss that has wreaked havoc on the Mexican economy.

No less an authority than Dr. H. J. Witteveen, former director of the International Monetary Fund, put it this way at a conference of central bankers recently convened in London:

> This [the dollar standard] system can be criticized, because foreign exchange reserves are created as a consequence of balance of payment deficits of the United States without any relationship to world reserve needs. Implicit in this is an unfair advantage to the reserve country, the United States, because it can finance its deficits by paying in its own currency. This makes it too easy to run deficits, and it creates an inflationary element in the monetary system, compared to the classical gold standard... By paying in its own currency, the United States could continue to finance enormous deficits without being forced to adequate deficit reducing measures.

Dr. Witteveen reports that U.S. dollar holdings by central banks have been reduced to 50 percent in recent years, and that figure is declining rapidly. At one time 95 percent of the world's trade was denominated in U.S. dollars. This raises some serious questions, not the least of which is what happens to the typical American investment portfolio if the dollar were to lose its reserve status. As you can see by Dr. Witteveen's comment, the international community is not favorably disposed to the American currency advantage. Such sentiments could be signaling major changes in the international financial system. In 1999, for example, Europe plans to introduce its own reserve currency, the euro. Speculation has already begun in financial circles as to what this portends for the dollar. Reviews thus far have not been favorable for the greenback. The dollar has already lost 74 percent of its purchasing power since 1971, and when that is coupled with the United States having become the largest debtor nation on earth, these rumblings from the international economic community sound ominous indeed.

You would be hard pressed to find a country in the world today that would have the wherewithal, or even the desire, to bail out the United States the way this country bailed out Mexico in 1995. On the contrary, most other nations would be scrambling to protect themselves in what could develop into a worldwide economic crash. American investors would be left to their own devices, using whatever means could be found to protect a rapidly evaporating balance sheet.

By the way, those of you who study millennial phenomena might be interested to know that Nostradamus also predicted the final seven years of the twentieth century would be a time of unprecedented social, economic, and ecological disasters—the darkest hours before the dawn of a new age. This prediction coincides with those of many Christian writers and thinkers who predict similar outcomes as we approach the year 2000. If the past is prologue, then we in the

United States should take heed of Nostradamus' warning. The problems with public debt could very well
lead to consequences as terrible as he predicts.

In 1945 the national debt stood at $260 billion, a
figure few fretted about because we had just fought a
war. Government-procured debt is generally considered a consequence of war. In the first five years after
the war, the debt was actually paid down some. This,
however, was only a brief interlude. Beginning in
1960 and stretching through 1995, there has not been
a single year when the national debt has been reduced, not even by a small amount. (See Figure 10.)
On the contrary, from Richard Nixon's presidency forward, the smallest annual growth rate was 3.8 percent
in 1974. The largest was a whopping 20.6 percent
growth in the national debt in 1983, the third year of
Ronald Reagan's presidency. In 1970, the accumulated
national debt equaled roughly one-third of the gross
national product. By 1995, it equaled 70 percent, a
virtually unsustainable progression. And that's not the
worst of it. The accumulated debt figure we hear so
much about does not include the massive spending
that has occurred "off budget." That figure in 1995
would have increased the deficit by over two and a
half times! Nor does it take into account the annual
raids on the Social Security trust fund carried out by
the politicians in Washington. D.C.

The net interest on this debt (at least the portion
the government acknowledges) approximates 17.5
percent of what the government collects in individual
and corporate taxes. Interest payments by the federal
government nearly equal what is spent on national
defense. The only figures that profoundly exceed net

Figure 10. Budget Deficits—
Nixon to Clinton Administrations

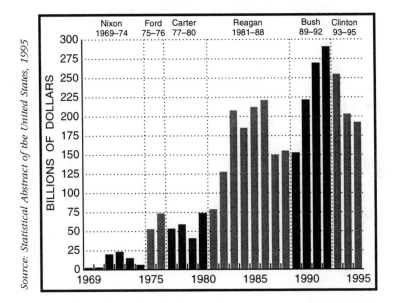

Source: Statistical Abstract of the United States, 1995

interest as a cost component of the federal budget are those for Medicare and Medicaid, programs many feel are at the root of the budget problem in the first place. No one knows what will happen to American society as a whole if interest rates double or even go up by 50 percent. Perhaps we do not want to know. It is too frightening a scenario.

Frightening it should be. The national debt, like Frankenstein's monster, has taken on a life of its own. Most have heard about the debt clock ticking upward at the rate of roughly $1 billion per day, averaging about $300 billion per year. But few have translated these figures to the personal level. The national debt now exceeds $5 trillion, or $20,000 for every man, woman, and child in the United States! That translates into a debt load of $80,000 or more for the typical American family. That debt load increases by roughly $5,000 annually, with no end in sight.

The Impact on American Investors

The impact of the national debt on each American citizen cannot be fully understood unless we first understand how it affects the dollar. As the debt rises, it drives down the purchasing power of the dollar. Inflation, despite political rhetoric to the contrary, has become a way of life in this country. Since 1971, the consumer price index has risen 382 percent. As I mentioned earlier, if the dollar were to lose its advantage as the world's reserve currency, the inflation problem could escalate beyond acceptable limits for most Americans.

These facts concerning the value of the dollar— more than any economic treatise, more than any documentary, more than any politician's speech—tell the story of what has happened to America. It tells why we are forced to two-income families; why we work five months of the year to pay our taxes; why the national savings rate is one of the worst in the Western world; why inflation is endemic in our society despite claims it is dead; why we can't seem to get anywhere despite our best-laid plans and hard work. As the dollar has deteriorated, so has the American lifestyle. Unfortunately, it appears this set of circumstances will not likely reverse itself anytime soon.

Government Debt Held by Foreigners

Government economists used to tell us that the national debt doesn't matter because we owe it to ourselves. That has changed. The United States is now the largest debtor nation on earth. No country runs even a close second. In 1996, foreign-held U.S. Treasury debt had expanded $130 billion over the previous twelve months—an astonishing surge of over 30 percent! An article by Randall Forsyth appeared at that time in *Barron's*, pointing out that foreign holdings "now substantially exceed the Fed's (Federal Reserve Bank's) own portfolio of Treasuries." Increasingly, our economic fate is in the hands of the foreign holders of our debt. "Without the foreign central bank purchases of treasuries," writes Mr. Forsyth, "the United States would face a currency crisis not unlike what Mexico went through a little over a year ago. The dollar would be substantially weaker and inflation substantially higher."

Debt Monetization: The Road to Inflation

Monetization and government finance are quite often written about in such arcane, highly specialized language that few—including other economists—understand what the writer is trying to convey. In simple terms, monetization amounts to nothing more than printing money. It works like this. When the federal government cannot find domestic or foreign buyers for its debt issue (usually because the interest rate is not high enough to attract lenders), the Federal Reserve Bank buys this debt and issues a check to the government. The government spends this money and in turn debases all the currency outstanding. This is a sophistication of a process first utilized by the Roman emperors. They would take Roman aureus into the treasury as tax payments, shave some gold off the edges, remelt the shavings and mint them into more coins. The debased coins and the new coins would then be recirculated as aureii. The quantity of gold in circulation was not increased, only the number of aureii. Since an increasing supply of aureii was chasing roughly the same amount of goods, the net result was one of the first forms of currency inflation. The modern Federal Reserve engages itself in much the same process when it monetizes debt.

The most likely times for inflationary outbursts are the 18-24 months following a presidential election. Fed chairmen, both Republican and Democrat, have a tendency to monetize more debt previous to a presidential election in order to keep interest rates down and the economy moving in the right direction. A rising inflation rate in the ensuing years is the direct cost. The greatest inflations have been those following elections. The 1973-74 outburst followed the 1972 election year. The 1977-79 outburst followed the 1976 election. Even during the disinflationary 1980s, the inflation rate jumped proportionately following the 1984 and 1988 elections. In 1992 a record $38 billion was monetized by the Fed belying claims by some political pundits that George Bush lost because the Fed failed to accommodate his re-election. By way of comparison $14 billion was monetized in 1990 and $24 billion in 1991. True to form, debt monetization increased in the years leading up to Bill Clinton's re-election in 1996. It remains to be seen whether the monetization will result in inflation down the road. If the current trend continues, the amount of printing press money being created in the 1990s as a percentage of total government receipts will approach rates last achieved in the 1970s.

In addition, monetization could greatly accelerate in the years to come because foreign central banks might become skittish about holding U.S. debt. This is why the Clinton administration went to great lengths to avoid default during the 1995-96 budget crises. A default—even short-term—would have caused U.S. Treasury paper ratings to plummet. As it is, bond rating services in both Europe and the United States have cast a wary eye on U.S. debt instruments. Some have even threatened to lower their ratings—a warning sign of things to come.

The Politics of Debt

The American political process today is characterized by the politics of debt, in which one group having claims on the government treasury contends with another group with claims of their own. The American people, who underwrite this debt, are essentially unrepresented in the process. This fact lies at the heart of discontent in the United States today. The political parties—the Democrats, who essentially represent the entitlement receivers, and the Republicans, who represent the subsidy-seeking major corporations—have lost all semblance of the ideals upon which the nation was founded.

Taylor Caldwell, in her book *Lion of God* on Paul of Tarsus, makes a telling observation about the Roman Empire during the early era of Christianity. This observation sounds hauntingly familiar to students of modern American politics:

> [Rome's] constitution was inevitably eroded by ambitious and wicked and lustful men, in whom patriotism had long died, and who saw their nation not as a Colossus of freedom in the world and a light to the nations, but an arena in which they could gain prizes and eventually crown themselves.

Few can read Ms. Caldwell's words without thinking about what goes on in modern-day Washington, D.C. History has shown time and again that private gold ownership is the antidote to the excesses of big government.

8

H is for...
History of Gold since 1971

> *History is philosophy learned from examples.*
> *—Thucydides*

The most significant events in the modern history of gold are the Gold Standard Act of 1900, by which the United States joined most of Europe in a gold-based economic system; the Federal Reserve Act of 1913 by which the United States entered upon the long road to severing the dollar's link to gold; Franklin Delano Roosevelt's devaluation of the dollar in the 1930s and the subsequent confiscation of gold; the Bretton Woods Agreement following World War II, which fixed the dollar to gold and the rest of the world's currencies to the dollar; and finally the abrogation of Bretton Woods and the further devaluation of the dollar during Richard Nixon's presidency in the early 1970s.

For our purposes, the modern economic era began in 1971. That year President Richard Nixon abandoned the Bretton Woods Agreement, devalued the dollar, raised the fixed price of gold fictitiously to $37.50, and slammed shut the gold window to stop an international run on the U.S. gold reserve. Previous to Nixon's actions, the United States had reduced its once prodigious gold hoard of over 20,000 tons to just a little over 8,000 tons in an effort to support the $35 international benchmark. Much of the U.S. hoard went overseas, particularly to Europe. Two years later, the U.S. government raised its fixed gold price to $42.22. The dollar was freed to float against the rest of the world's currencies. Gold began to trade freely in gold markets around the world. Nixon's actions also gave a green light to uninhibited budget and trade deficits.

The United States is no longer required to deliver gold to any nation that steps up to the gold window and demands gold for dollars. In subsequent years, this would become the political equivalent of a license to inflate—something this country subscribes to with a vengeance. To this day, the U.S. gold reserve of roughly 260 billion ounces ostensibly is valued at $42.22 per ounce, despite the fact that the free market price is closer to $400. At the time, Richard Nixon proclaimed "We are all Keynesians." This was his way of saying that the forces of sound money were no longer to be represented in American politics, not even by the hard money and conservatively inclined Republican Party. With the abrogation of the Bretton Woods Agreement—the international economic structure erected after World War II based on gold—the foundation was simultaneously laid for the modern private gold market. When politicians took gold out of the national money, which is what Nixon did, the need for private gold ownership was enhanced as a means to protect wealth.

By 1973, gold climbed to $120 as price inflation gripped the nation. In that year, the federal debt stood at $466 billion, small by today's standards and representing only 34 percent of the gross domestic product. Double-digit inflation plagued the American economy in 1974. The stock market corrected significantly. That year Richard Nixon resigned from office under the pale of the Watergate scandal. The gold price hit $200, 5.5 times the price targeted in the late 1960s as gold's benchmark.

The recession years of 1975 and 1976 saw gold in a downtrend, bottoming out at $104. Jimmy Carter was elected president. Continued loose monetary policies, deficit spending, and an embargo against the United States by the Organization of Petroleum Exporting Countries exacerbated an already fragile international monetary situation. Inflation dominated the financial scene. The International Monetary Fund and the United States launched monthly gold auctions in 1975. Publicly, the government announced that the sales were intended to meet the newly generated demand resulting from the legalization of private gold ownership in the United States. The real reasons for the sales were to demonetize gold once and for all and to keep the price below $150. Nearly 1,200 tones of metal were expended by the IMF and the U.S. Treasury to no avail. By 1977, the price broke out again. In 1978 it was trading in the $250 range. Since the U.S. Treasury and IMF sales were having no effect on the gold price, the sales were curtailed in 1978. Gold went through the roof, making progress toward its all-time high. By 1979, the nation and the world had become engulfed in a full-blown monetary crisis. Gold peaked at $875 in a buying frenzy.

Ronald Reagan, vowing to bring stability to a troubled nation, was elected president in 1980, unseating the troubled incumbent Jimmy Carter. Interest rates hit 19 percent, an unheard-of level. But this cooled the gold market and brought stability to the dollar. In 1983, in what turned out to be a minor currency crisis in Europe resulting from the stronger dollar, gold investment demand drove the price back up to $500 after bottoming at just below $300 in 1982. Also in that year, the United States posted its highest unemployment rate since 1941. The American economy had entered an era of high interest rates, high unemployment, and a subdued, yet still high, inflation rate. This combination of factors has come to be known as *disinflation*. These circumstances still dominate the financial markets in the mid-1990s. A combination of high real interest rates (yields minus the inflation rate) and an abundance of oil has kept the inflation rate in check and the gold price from climbing radically. Gold bottomed in 1985 just below the $300 level. The national debt went over $2 trillion for the first time in 1986 and amounted to 50 percent of the annual gross national product—a very disturbing benchmark. Seventy banks failed in 1987 the most since the Great Depression, and the United States crossed the line to become the greatest debtor nation on earth. The stock market crashed, gold shot back up to $500. The world's central banks, in concert with the mining companies, began another assault on gold, driving it down quickly to the $350 level.

George Bush became president in 1988 and was immediately greeted by the worst banking crisis in U.S. history. In what came to be known as the S&L crisis, $300 billion was committed to bailing out mismanaged and sometimes fraudulently run savings and loan institutions. The national debt went over the $3 trillion mark, just three years after breaking the $2 trillion figure. By 1990 the economy was again in recession. For the first time since 1980, the United States posted a negative gross domestic product. The Soviet Union broke up, forever altering the international political landscape. Germany reunified. The United States subdued Sadam Hussein and Iraq in the Gulf War, the highlight of George Bush's presidency. Some said the Cold War had come to an end. In the United States, massive back-to-back deficits pushed the accumulated federal debt over $4 trillion, just two years after breaking the $3 trillion mark.

In 1992 the United States ran its biggest deficit in history—$290 billion. Gold remained in the doldrums under the influence of continuing official sales and pressure from the mining companies selling their production forward. Gold was driven back toward the $300 mark, bottoming at $330 as Bill Clinton was inaugurated president. Pushed by a Japanese banking crisis, a monetary crisis in Europe, and the belief that Bill Clinton's administration would rekindle an inflationary economy, resurgent gold demand pushed the price up to $425. Gold production began to fall, while demand for gold reached record levels worldwide, particularly in the Far East. Only record forward sales by the mines and official central bank sales (detailed in Chapter 6) kept the price from bolting higher. In

1995 the United States, mired in economic problems of its own, bailed out Mexico. The federal government shut down during a budget battle between the Republican controlled U.S. Congress and the Clinton administration. Gold began to rise again in early 1996, once again challenging the $425 mark. The national debt went past $5 trillion, a figure representing over 70 percent of the gross domestic product. As 1996 drew to a close, gold returned to the $370 level under pressure from heavy forward sales by South African mining companies.

The history of gold teaches us that governments, including our own, cannot be trusted to manage money. What's more, in lieu of proper management of treasuries, today's governments have tended to focus on artificially controlling the gold price, rather than putting forth policies that would bolster the currency's value.

Historically, gold's value has been universally understood while the value of government paper, in the absence of gold backing, is nearly always subject to question. It is important to understand that there is more to the gold market than the basic supply and demand fundamentals that characterize other commodities. Gold, beyond the fundamentals, is a very political investment, and understanding its history adds to understanding its place now in one's portfolio.

The following annotated graphs tell this short history of gold since 1971 and show the important economic and political events that have accompanied gold's erratically upward climb. Study them well, for gold's history is our own.

Figure 11. History of Gold 1968 to 1975

DOLLARS

$183.85

1972-73
R. Nixon devalues dollar again.
Official gold price = $42.22/oz.
Arab oil embargo. Watergate.
Gold breaks out, hits $120 in
June, 1973. Gross U.S. federal
debt = $466 billion, or 34% of GNP.

1971
R. Nixon devalues dollar.
Wage and price controls.
Inflation rate rises.
Fed Reserve closes gold
window, ending $ convertibility.
Official gold price = $38/oz.
Viet Nam war intensifies.

1969-70
London Gold Pool abandoned.
Foreign central banks begin
to drain U.S. gold reserve.

1967-68
London Gold Pool formed
to maintain official $35 gold price.
Sell 2,000+ tons over two years
nearly doubling supply.

1974
Worldwide double-digit inflation.
Stock market collapses. Gold peaks
at 5.5 x Gold Pool price of $35.
Nixon resigns.

1975
King Faisal killed.
OPEC raises oil prices again.
Recession sets in.
Gold begins correction.

1968 1969 1970 1971 1972 1973 1974 1975

0 20 40 60 80 100 120 140 160 180 200

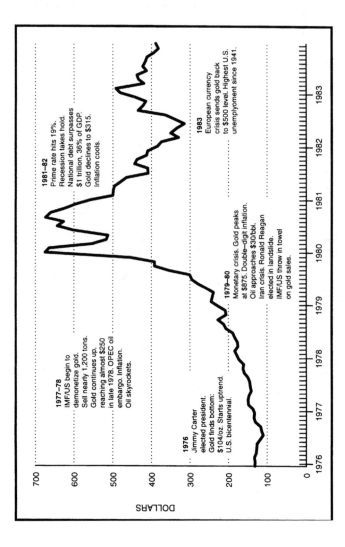

Figure 12. History of Gold 1976 to 1983

1976
Jimmy Carter
elected president.
Gold finds bottom:
$104/oz. Starts uptrend.
U.S. bicentennial.

1977–78
IMF/US begin to
demonetize gold.
Sell nearly 1,200 tons.
Gold continues up,
reaching almost $250
in late 1978. OPEC oil
embargo. Inflation.
Oil skyrockets.

1979–80
Monetary crisis. Gold peaks
at $875. Double–digit inflation.
Oil approaches $30/bbl.
Iran crisis. Ronald Reagan
elected in landslide.
IMF/US throw in towel
on gold sales.

1981–82
Prime rate hits 19%.
Recession takes hold.
National debt surpasses
$1 trillion, 36% of GDP.
Gold declines to $315.
Inflation cools.

1983
European currency
crisis sends gold back
to $500 level. Highest U.S.
unemployment since 1941.

Figure 13. **History of Gold 1984 to 1991**

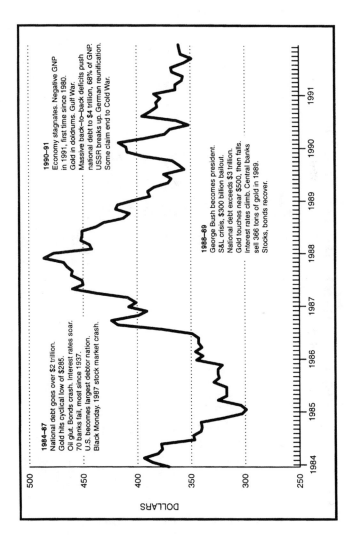

1984–87
National debt goes over $2 trillion.
Gold hits cyclical low of $285.
Oil glut. Bonds crash. Interest rates soar.
70 banks fail, most since 1937.
U.S. becomes largest debtor nation.
Black Monday. 1987 stock market crash.

1988–89
George Bush becomes president.
S&L crisis, $300 billion bailout.
National debt exceeds $3 trillion.
Gold touches near $500, then falls.
Interest rates climb. Central banks
sell 366 tons of gold in 1989.
Stocks, bonds recover.

1990–91
Economy stagnates. Negative GNP
in 1991, first time since 1980.
Gold in doldrums. Gulf War.
Massive back–to–back deficits push
national debt to $4 trillion, 68% of GNP.
USSR breaks up. German reunification.
Some claim end to Cold War.

DOLLARS

500 450 400 350 300 250

1984 1985 1986 1987 1988 1989 1990 1991

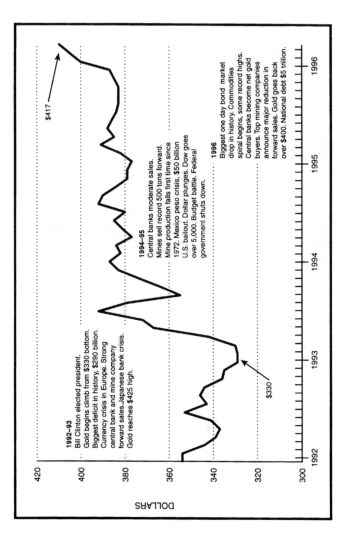

Figure 14. History of Gold 1992 to 1996

1992–93
Bill Clinton elected president.
Gold begins climb from $330 bottom.
Biggest deficit in history, $290 billion.
Currency crisis in Europe. Strong
central bank and mine company
forward sales. Japanese bank crisis.
Gold reaches $425 high.

1994–95
Central banks moderate sales.
Mines sell record 500 tons forward.
Mine production falls first time since
1972. Mexico peso crisis, $50 billion
U.S. bailout. Dollar plunges. Dow goes
over 5,000. Budget battle. Federal
government shuts down.

1996
Biggest one day bond market
drop in history. Commodities
spiral begins, some record highs.
Central banks become net gold
buyers. Top mining companies
announce major reduction in
forward sales. Gold goes back
over $400. National debt $5 trillion.

$417

$330

DOLLARS

420 400 380 360 340 320 300

1992   1993   1994   1995   1996

9

I is for...
The Inflation/Deflation Debate:
Either Way, Gold Is a Winner

Ever since Richard Nixon took the United States (and the world) off the gold standard in 1971, an ongoing debate has been waged between those who believe the American economy is headed for an hyperinflationary breakdown and those who believe that a deflationary collapse is inevitable. Volumes have been written espousing both scenarios. Newsletter writers seem to be divided evenly on the subject. History shows gold, better than any other asset, protects against both calamities.

At times (like the 1970s) the inflationists have appeared to be right. At other times (like the early 1990s), the deflationists have appeared to be right. Thus far we have escaped either extreme. Instead of inflation followed by deflation, we have had inflationary episodes followed by disinflationary or stagflationary episodes wherein the inflation rate has simply been moderated. Today's inflation rate, for example, was enough for Richard Nixon to impose wage and price controls on the economy in 1972. Now it is considered to be a sign that inflation is under control. The lesson is, there is little doubt the underlying trend in the American economy is inflationary. How this situation is likely to resolve itself is the subject of a great deal of discussion.

Deflationists argue that the public and private debt now on the books is approaching $20 trillion and it can never be sustained or paid off. They say it will be liquidated through default. As bankruptcies mount, banks will fail. Fearful investors will scramble to unload their stocks and bonds. A crash ensues. In such a scenario, gold becomes the asset of last resort and possibly the only asset other than cash ($100 bills) worth owning. Some analysts predict gold prices in the thousands of dollars in such scenarios.

Inflationists paint a different picture. The Federal Reserve could be forced to print money (monetize debt) in ever increasing increments to keep the government in operation. This paper blizzard will wend its way through the economy, pushing prices higher and higher. Exporters to the United States, particularly oil exporters, will be forced to continuously ratchet up prices to receive real value for their oil. Since oil is the lifeblood of the economy and is a cost component of just about everything we consume, all prices will be pushed higher still. Inflation will begin to compound itself. The situation will become exacerbated, much like what occurred in the late 1970s, only this time it gets out of control. Hyperinflation ensues, and gold skyrockets.

No one knows off which side of the tightwire—hyperinflation or deflationary crash—the economy will fall. Needless to say, neither proposition is very comforting from an investor's point of view. Yet from the point of view of the gold investor, the inflation/deflation debate is purely academic. Gold will protect and preserve your assets in either instance. Gold is the time-honored, historically proven hedge against economic disasters of all descriptions.

Both deflationists and inflationists recommend gold as *the* portfolio item to hedge against disaster. In a deflationary crash, gold becomes the only asset left standing after all others are destroyed by default. In an inflationary debacle, gold survives the destruction of the currency and retains its value after all other assets are wiped out. Hedge your portfolio with gold and leave the inflation/deflation argument to the economists.

10

J is for...
Judgment of History: We Are Not Immune

Highly placed sources in banking and business circles in
Europe and South America warn that unless the U.S.
government moves quickly to control the spending which is
ballooning the deficit, America is imminent danger of South
American, banana Republic style hyperinflation.
—Jack Anderson, political columnist

Historians teach us that civilizations go through cycles of birth, growth, decline, and death much like
a biological organism. Though some would now have
you believe America is somehow immune from this
process, history teaches us differently. Historical cycles—the ebb and flow of change—are the primary facts
of life on this planet. Currency debasement is a prominent feature of an empire's decline. The examples are
numerous. Rome. Greece. Genghis Khan. Napoleonic
France. Post-World War II Britain. So to think we are
somehow immune from this process seems to be a bit
arrogant, especially in view of the fact that the United

States is currently in the midst of a currency debasement of its own.

Thomas Jefferson, in his sage years at Monticello, said, if it were possible he would amend the U.S. Constitution to prohibit the government from borrowing money—that is, running deficits. "It is vain," said Jefferson with regard to government debt, "for common sense to urge that nothing can produce nothing; that is an idle dream to believe in, a philosopher's stone which turns everything into gold."

Under Richard Nixon, as I pointed out earlier, the largest deficit was $23.4 billion; under Jimmy Carter, $73.8 billion; under Ronald Reagan, $221.2 billion; and under George Bush, $290.2 billion. Bill Clinton in his first year in office ran a $290 billion deficit with the help of a Democratic Congress and had the gall to proclaim it a victory against government profligacy. It will not be long until deficits could exceed the $500 billion mark, budget battles notwithstanding. This, to understate the problem, is a frightening progression.

The corollary to government deficits, if history is a teacher, is inflation followed by severe economic contraction. We need look no further than the post-World War I German inflation for a stark example. At its height, a family's life savings could not purchase a cup of coffee. The inflation disaster in Germany during the 1920s led to depression and finally paved the way for Adolf Hitler and Nazism.

No one knows for certain where the United States now stands relative to the cycles of civilization, though many historians have warned the situation looks precarious. No one knows for certain whether we need to prepare for the Great American Inflation

or the next Great American Depression. Nor does anyone know whether the problems that have befallen
this country will result in its decline and fall. We do
know, however, that history is neither prejudicial nor
selective. For some reason, many Americans like to
believe that somehow America will escape its judg-
ment. It is both foolish and arrogant to believe "it"
can't happen here. It *can* happen here. In fact, many
contend it *is* happening here.

11

K is for...
Know Thyself

Without waxing philosophical, a few words are helpful concerning the mind-set with which you pursue your interest in gold ownership. Some enter the gold market to make a profit, others to hedge disaster, some to accomplish both. No matter into which category you fit, make sure you understand why you are going into the gold market. Convey that understanding to the individual with whom you are structuring your gold portfolio. The *whys* have quite a bit to do with *what* you end up owning.

Frequently investors will say that any kind of gold will do because after all gold is gold, *isn't it?* This type of attitude has helped a great many coin shop owners unload unwanted inventory they hadn't been able to get rid of for years. This is probably a good deal for the coin dealer, but it could spell disaster for you. In the same vein, I have talked to hundreds, probably thousands, of investors in nearly a quarter century in the business. Quite often, potential investor's have no more reason for buying gold than "everybody else is doing it."

In Chapter 16 on portfolio planning, you will find some details on this important subject. For now, consider the inscription over the entrance to the temple of the ancient Delphic Oracle: "Know Thyself." Study. Read. Learn what's going on around you. Call a few gold firms and ask questions. There's nothing like conversation to stimulate thinking. Take time to lay a little groundwork. Then make your move. The political and economic situation being what it is, there is no better time to start than now. Know thyself—your goals and needs—and you will be a more confident, happier gold investor.

12

L is for...

London, New York, Hong Kong, Zurich: A Day in the Life of the Gold Market

> *Real gold is not afraid of the fire of a red furnace.*
> —*Chinese proverb*

Even as you read this section, a gold price is being posted somewhere in the world. Like the old British empire, the sun never sets on the gold market. (See Figure 15.) For centuries, gold has captured the imagination of those with a "trading mentality" who dare to buy here and sell there with the hope of making a profit in the bargain. Now with the advent of computer screens, satellite transmissions, and faxed buy/sell confirmations, the gold market has been internationalized. It is not unusual for a trader in New York to take a position on the London market as he eats breakfast and then sell that position in Australia as he prepares to retire in the evening.

For American gold traders, the day begins in London. Before traders on the East Coast have had their first cup of coffee, the five members of the London gold market have agreed upon their morning gold fix. They have assessed supply and demand for that day and have established a price they believe will adequately match the buys and sells streaming in from mining companies, bullion dealers and traders, central banks, internationally based commercial banks, refiners, and commercial brokerages. If the buys exceed the sells in sufficient quantity, the price is raised. If vice versa, the price is lowered.

In recent years London has become an increasingly important center for the gold trade, making headway toward its old place at the head of the gold trading table lost to COMEX in New York and to the Zurich market. The reason? London is where the world's central banks have set up shop for their gold lending operations to mining companies. (See Chapter 6.) The volumes in London are substantial. Terry Smeeton, head of gold and foreign exchange operations for the Bank of England, estimates the volume in London is 7.5 million ounces daily, currently 50 percent higher than COMEX. The London market offers both spot and forward sales. *Spot sales* represent gold sold at the posted London price. *Forward sales* represent gold sold by contract in the future at an agreed-upon price, with the London market serving as the go-between.

The five men who set the London fixes represent some of the largest, oldest, and most influential banks and gold dealers in the world: N.M. Rothschild (which provides the group's chairman), Midland Bank (formerly Samuel Montague), Deutsch Bank Sharps Pixley, Republic National Bank of New York (the American entry in 1994), and Mocatta Group (formerly Mocatta Goldschmidt, the oldest member, founded in 1671). They set two fixes each day. The morning fix is set at 10:30 London time, known in the industry as the A.M. fix. This is the one usually announced on American radio networks as you drive to work in the morning. The afternoon fix is set after lunch and is known as the P.M. fix. The five men meet in the offices of N.M. Rothschild under the watchful eye of founder Nathan Rothschild, whose portrait hangs appropriately in the conservatively appointed trading room. All business is done under the London Code of Conduct for bullion dealers. Only gentlemen need apply.

COMEX in New York opens at 8:20 A.M. eastern time and begins operations while the London market is still open. The highly charged auction market atmosphere of COMEX stands in stark contrast to the restrained, dignified arrangements made in London. We have all seen the video clips—traders shouting at each other, waving their arms, pointing fingers, making hand signals— a picture of seeming confusion and anarchy. Interestingly, throughout the apparent chaos runs a thread of perfect order. Buys and sells are actually matched and prices set. Typically, traders in the "pit" are young men and women for an obvious reason: the frenzy takes its toll.

From 1933, when Franklin Roosevelt confiscated gold, until 1975, when Gerald Ford signed legislation legalizing it, gold did not trade formally in the United States. As the dollar began its long descent following

Richard Nixon's devaluations in 1971 in 1973, gold began to take on a certain amount of appeal among traders and investors in the United States. COMEX grew with the American market and forever changed the international gold scene. COMEX during the 1970s and 1980s was *the* dominant gold market in terms of setting the daily prices. London now challenges the predominance of COMEX because of its mine company and central bank activity. COMEX is likely to regain predominance when more private investors return to the market.

COMEX operates on a spacious trading floor in the World Trade Center in New York City. Gold contracts are for 100 ounces. They trade daily between 8:20 A.M. and 2:30 P.M. eastern time. The COMEX price is the one used by gold firms across the United States as a base for pricing bullion and bullion coins. Most firms have satellite hookups to COMEX to which they refer continuously during the business day. "COMEX price" and "New York price" are terms often used interchangeably by many gold firms. In 1993, when interest in the gold market rekindled, COMEX volumes and open interest moved to substantially higher levels. Since then these levels have been maintained, reflecting a strong ongoing interest in gold despite relatively stable prices.

After New York closes, interest centers around what has come to be known as the California after-market. Quite often California traders take their cue from the Australian market, one that has grown with mine production in that country. California is not a large-volume market, but it reflects the amount of interest in an on-going trend—down or up. It is therefore useful for traders who need to know whether a trend might extend itself around the globe.

The Hong Kong market opens after Australia's. This market first traded gold in 1910, when British banks thought they might need a mechanism for trading gold in the Orient. Today it is the launch site for gold going to mainland China, one of the fastest-growing gold markets in the world. In fact, the whole Asian market has been so active in recent years that American and European gold traders who travel there talk about it in wistful tones normally reserved for the American market of the late 1970s and early 1980s. This market is highly influential in Asia, because Hong Kong is where Japanese investors, banks, and financial houses occasionally hedge their orders. It is also in a time zone that fits nicely with the business day of traders in Saudi Arabia and the rest of the Persian

Figure 15. A Day in the Life of the Gold Market

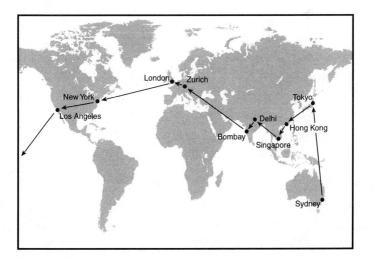

Gulf. If Hong Kong is moving, it is quite often due to the buying or selling of the Middle East. Large amounts of Hong Kong gold are also made into jewelry for export throughout Asia. For the most part, Hong Kong serves as a convenient midway point in the trading day because it fills the gap between markets in the United States and Europe.

In The *World of Gold*, expert Timothy Green characterizes the Hong Kong market this way:

They [the Hong Kong traders] like awkward tael-weight bars [based on 1.2-ounce units] and resist suggestions that they should trade in ounces and U.S. dollars to conform to world patterns. They delayed for years the introduction of the Reuters monitor computer system, fearing a computer must invade the secrecy of their "society."

For the most part, these sentiments do not sound foreign at all to many American gold owners.

The next market to open in gold's day is Zurich, Switzerland. This market is dominated by the big three Swiss banks—Swiss Bank Corporation, Swiss Credit Bank, and Union Bank of Switzerland. They first made a splash in the world gold market by convincing South Africa that they would be better merchants for its gold than London, particularly since the Swiss banks would be the end buyers themselves instead of acting as intermediaries like the London banks. Then, in the early 1970s, Russia—the second largest producer (South Africa was first) at the time—began to ship its gold to Switzerland. Zurich in this way became the largest dealer of *physical* gold bullion in the world shipping to all corners of the globe. Now, as Timothy Green has put it, "Gold is as much a part of Switzerland as the Alps and skiing." Switzerland appeals to a great many of the world's gold mega-hoarders. Many individuals who do not trust their own governments admire Switzerland for its secrecy laws and its long history of judiciously handling other people's money. As a result, much of the world's privately held gold is stored secretly in Swiss vaults.

The London market opens while Zurich is still trading. It quite often takes its cue from Zurich. So goes gold around the world each day.

13

M is for...
Myths and Realities about Gold

Gold has its critics. Yet most of their criticism is ill founded and amounts to little more than good propaganda for those who fear strong gold demand will divert investor interest from the equities markets and the dollar. You have probably heard or read most of the standard criticisms. Here are concise and complete rebuttals—the last words on the merits of gold.

Myth: Gold is not a good portfolio item because it doesn't pay interest.

Reality: That gold does not pay interest is its greatest strength. If gold were to pay interest, it would mean the return *on* your gold and the return *of* your gold would be dependent on the performance of another individual or institution. This, of course, is the case with paper assets such as bonds, bank certified deposits, even stocks. The contractual relationship between the creditor and debtor can be a paper asset's greatest strength. It can also be its greatest weakness. An additional and often complicating factor is that paper assets are directly affected by the performance of the currencies in which they are denominated.

Gold, on the other hand, is a stand-alone investment independent of government largesse or the performance of another individual or institution. This is gold's greatest strength. Even though gold does not pay interest directly, as its critics claim, it is interesting to note that over any extended period of time the interest rate of currency becomes imputed in the price. During inflationary periods the appreciation in the price of gold is the greatest, and so is the rise in interest rates. During deflationary periods the gold price tends to stay flat while interest rates plummet. Gold historically seeks a price level that takes into account the inflation rate of currency. This compensates for its non-interest-bearing status.

Myth: Gold stocks are a better portfolio option than gold itself.

Reality: Gold stocks are stocks first and gold second. This is an important distinction for investors to recognize because, once it is understood, justifying gold *stock* ownership as a substitute for gold itself becomes very difficult. Owning gold stocks is not unlike owning other types of stock. As a matter of fact, in the last three stock market crashes—1929, 1935, and 1987—gold stocks also tumbled into the abyss, belying claims by stockbrokers that they can serve as a hedge against disaster.

In addition, you could presumably own a gold stock during a period of rising gold prices and not participate in the uptrend simply because a company had diminishing prospects in the eyes of the investment community. Another problem with gold stocks in the 1990s is that many mining companies have sold several years of production forward as part of their mine financing programs. If the price of gold rises, these companies could be excluded from the bull market because they will have already sold their production forward at prices less, even considerably less, than the current market rate. Gold stocks are not an investment in gold. They are simply another stock market investment and should be analyzed as such. There is no substitute for owning the real thing.

Myth: Gold is just another commodity, like pork bellies.

Reality: Gold trades on the commodities exchanges along with pork bellies and the other commodities, but here the similarity ends. Unlike other commodities, which are produced strictly for consumption, gold is the only commodity that is *accumulated and saved.* It is also the only commodity used as money to facilitate future consumption. Most of the gold ever produced still exists today. You cannot say the same thing about pork bellies, soybeans, or sugar. The gold you might someday purchase could very well have been part of the treasury of Rome, or used by Marco Polo in his first visit to China, or circulated as currency in the Old West. This money (asset preservation) function of gold separates it from the commodity complex and gives it a special place at the very top of the value scale.

Those who relegate gold to the status of "just another commodity" usually do so because they either fear gold or do not like competing against it. By denigrating it, they hope to subdue public accumulation—an exercise in futility. Gold is *the* enduring commodity.

Myth: Gold is a "barbarous relic" of past monetary systems, irrelevant in today's computerized markets.

Reality: Gold is held as a reserve asset in nearly every central bank in the world. It serves as their asset of last resort, to be used for grave international crises such as war, economic troubles, environmental disasters, and the like. Former U.S. Federal Reserve Chairman Paul Volcker recently made these comments about gold and central banking, answering the "barbarous relic" claims:

> We sometimes forget that central banking as we know it today is, in fact, largely an invention of the past hundred years or so, even though a few central banks can trace their ancestry back to the early nineteenth century or before. It is a sobering fact that the prominence of central banks in this century has coincided with a general tendency toward more inflation, not less. By and large, if the overriding objective is price stability, we did better with the nineteenth century gold standard and passive central banks, with currency boards, or even with "free banking." The truly unique power of a central bank, after all, is the power to create money, and ultimately the power to create is the power to destroy.

Other central bankers, including current U.S. Federal Reserve Chairman Alan Greenspan, have voiced similar admiration for this "barbarous relic." In lieu of an international gold standard, individual investors have been forced to place themselves on the gold standard even in today's computerized markets. Gold today has the same relevance it has always enjoyed. It is the asset of last resort and universal value for both individual investors and nation-states.

Myth: World governments in conjunction with their central banks control the gold price. They intend to hold that price down.

Reality: In each instance in modern monetary history when governments and central banks (including our own federal government and central bank) acted to hold the gold price down, the price was on the verge of moving substantially higher due to inflationary policies these very same institutions were promulgating. Their activities to hold gold down amounted to exercises in futility, only delaying the dominant, underlying trend. As a matter of fact, government interventions in the gold market in the past (most recently in the 1960s and 1970s) have amounted to no less than solid indicators that the price was about to go substantially higher. Far from being able to control gold, to the consternation of some central bankers and governments, they too must answer ultimately to what the gold market is telling them. When it comes to currency value, gold is the master of all and a slave of none.

Myth: Gold is a speculative, volatile investment that should be avoided by conservative investors.

Reality: It is not gold that changes in value, but currencies. What you could purchase with an ounce of gold a hundred years ago you can purchase with an ounce of gold today. The reason for the spikes dominating the gold charts is not gold's volatility but, rather government and/or central bank intervention to suppress the price. Once market forces overcame the intervention, gold sought its natural level, which proved to be multiples of the interventionists' target range. Hence the spikes. If the interventionists had not acted to keep gold down, the chart would have shown a more gradual rise, and gold's critics would be unable to make claims of its volatility.

Myth: Gold is an unpatriotic investment.

Reality: It has become a small world. Investors now invest their money in economies all over the world. Is it unpatriotic for an investor to buy Swiss annuities, or a Japanese equities fund, or a South American gold fund? Would this be considered un-American? Probably not. There is also the question of whether citizens are obligated to lose everything they have holding a currency that is being systematically debased by the government and its monetary authorities. As I have shown in other sections of this book, the monetary policies of the United States virtually assure further devaluation of the dollar in the future.

The world's central banks have already responded to these circumstances by substantially reducing their holdings of dollars, not too long ago the chief international reserve currency. No one knows the long-term outcome of such a transformation, but few who understand the problem feel they should go unprotected. Far from being unpatriotic, citizens who accumulate gold may be the exact opposite. They could very well turn out to be the country's most farsighted, devoted, and *patriotic* resource. Indeed, the fact that certain citizens have the wisdom to accumulate gold may someday turn out to be this country's saving grace. If the dollar were to fail, the gold accumulated in the United States by American citizens would become the capital base required for this nation to recover—a thought worth pondering.

14

N is for...
Numismatics: A Diversification Within a Diversification, or a Stand-Alone Vehicle for Growth

Numismatics—investing in rare U.S. coins—is not for every investor. The bull markets can be incredibly lucrative. The bear markets can be devastating. No investor should acquire truly rare coins as an ultimate hedge against disaster simply because they might be difficult to liquidate in an emergency. If you can accept the volatile nature of the market as both its greatest detriment as well as its greatest attribute, then perhaps investing in rare coins is something you should pursue. Be sure you find an experienced adviser. This is not the type of thing most investors can do on their own. Those who try usually regret not having gone with an expert. It is well worth paying an expert who can act as your ally and confidant in this market.

Investors looking to protect themselves against economic disasters should first build a foundation of gold bullion coins and/or pre-1933 $20 gold pieces.

(This is covered in more detail in Chapter 16.) Once that foundation is complete, adding rare coins to your portfolio as a growth vehicle is warranted. Rare coins historically have participated in major precious metals rallies, especially if the rallies are inflation induced. In Germany during the 1920s, when hyperinflation destroyed the mark, substantial assets were saved—and profits won—by investments in numismatics.

Rare coins are a minimum three- to five-year investment. The market tends to move in fits and starts. Steady appreciation is as rare as the coins in which you are investing. On the other hand, in the long run coins have an impressive record and historically perform in a way very similar to the stock market. If you go into it with the attitude that you are in the investment for the long run, you will probably do just fine. (Of course, there are no guarantees.) On the other hand, if you do not have the financial and psychological staying power, the market could teach you one of those lessons you would like to forget. The rare coin market consists of sectors, much like the stock market. There are silver dollars, small-denomination gold coins, nineteenth century coins, twentieth century coins, and so forth. Like stocks, these sectors tend to attract and repel interest. A sector can sit dormant for years before moving in either direction. Once it starts moving, the action can be fast and furious. Quite often a sector can double in a single year and then go into dormancy again, or even go down just as rapidly. This market is not for the fainthearted. If you go into the investment realizing that the holding period is at least three to five years, you stand a good chance of being in the market when it does spike. You might not see any appreciation for the first two years. You might then experience a doubling in the third year, for example, which makes for a nice profit. Patience and tenacity are the keys to success.

Two other factors figure greatly in the success of a numismatic investment: grade and population. *Grade* refers to the quality of the coin. The grading system for investment-grade items starts, in my opinion, with mint state (proof) 64 coins and goes to mint state 70. There are few or no coins today in the mint state 70 designation. Do not purchase coins below mint state 64 unless the item is a recognized rarity. It is better to own one scarce or rare mint state 65, 66, or 67 coin in a series than a dozen mint state 63 coins in the same series. Many large marketing organizations in the field push low-grade (mint state 63 or less) coins as numismatic investments. But the pros in the field consider these items common, not worthy of the appellation *investment*. As a result, when the investment houses are "out of the market," which happens frequently, these items are severely discounted. The investor bears the brunt of the devaluation. Scarce and rare coins, on the other hand, enjoy the benefit of a large common-sense market. In this market, the greater the rarity, the better the value in the long run. Any comparative review of price histories in any sector of the coin market bears out this observation.

When purchasing rare coins, make sure they have been graded by either the Numismatic Guaranty Corporation or the Professional Coin Grading Service and are housed in hard plastic containers. This increases their liquidity and narrows the spread. Avoid all other grading services and purchasing coins that have not been graded by one of these independent services.

Population is the other key factor in numismatic investments. This refers to the number of coins given a specific grade by the grading services. When purchasing rare coins, check into their relative rarity (population figure) against other items in the series or sector. Both grading services publish "population reports," which provide this data. Stick with strong, relative rarity or scarcity. It pays in the long run and increases the likelihood your purchase(s) will be among the beneficiaries if there is a run-up in value for that series.

A couple of additional advantages of coin investing are worth mentioning. There are no reporting requirements for buying or selling, so your privacy is easily maintained. You can trade numismatic items as "like kind exchanges," thus delaying capital gains taxes until you liquidate. This allows you to build strong asset value by trading appreciated sectors for sectors that have remained dormant in the hope they will be the next to move upward. Rare coins are excellent wealth builders. A great many investors enter the field of numismatic investing simply for this advantage.

Be aware that the coin market is notoriously thin. It is characterized by both steep run-ups and steep declines. The thin market also creates large spreads between buying and selling when it is in decline and better spreads when it is going up. In a weak market, the selling compounds itself as the coins seek strong hands. In a strong market, it is sometimes (but not always) difficult to find the better items because investors tend to "hold out." In numismatics the byword is patience in both buying and selling. Never allow yourself to feel pressed. If you are forced to sell at the wrong time, you will be at the mercy of the market.

Taken in the right context, coin investing can be both fun and profitable. In the late 1970s and the mid-to-late 1980s, the coin market experienced explosive rallies, producing profits three to seven times the base starting point according to some analysts. So there is no denying the potential. The coin market has been in a long bear market. Many rare items can be purchased at fractions of their late 1980s' prices, when the coin market last peaked. Now it appears the market is making a bottom. Profit-seeking investors might consider a modest commitment while the market is low. Once again, hedge investors should start with bullion coins and pre-1933 $20 gold pieces and work their way toward numismatics once a foundation is built.

15

O is for...
Other Precious Metals

No discussion of gold investing would be complete without at least a few words about gold's close relatives—silver and platinum. Gold's importance as a portfolio item lies primarily in its monetary value. It is a store of value first and a commodity second, even though it has performed well from a commodity perspective in the past. With silver and platinum, the situation is reversed. Both are commodities first and stores of value second. They tend to do well in inflationary economies—sometimes phenomenally well—but can severely deflate in a depression. For these reasons, silver and platinum play an important secondary role in portfolio planning as a way to speculate against the dollar when the inflationary fires are fanned. Neither of these metals should be used as a deflationary hedge.

Silver and platinum are neither permanent nor semi-permanent members of the portfolio family. Rather, they are to be gleaned once profits have been made. One option is to convert profitable platinum and silver holdings to gold, once you feel these metals have had their run. In past bull markets, even in mini-bull markets, silver and platinum have outperformed gold percentage-wise. A correct call could help you end up with more gold in the long run than if you had purchased only gold to begin with. These metals are particularly useful to wealthy individuals who have sufficient gold reserves and would now like to branch out into something with stronger profit potential. For most, though, it is important to build a gold reserve first because it will get you through bad times no matter what the dominant economic trend. Keep in mind the risk/reward ratio: the upside could be greater with silver and platinum, but so could the downside. The swings of these two metals are much more significant than those of gold. Be forewarned.

Since both metals rely on their commodity values for future appreciation, the most important factors are the supply/demand fundamentals. Let's briefly review each, starting with silver.

Silver

According to statistics supplied by the Silver Institute, 40 percent of the world's silver supply comes from Mexico, Peru, and the former Soviet Union. Mine production has been in steady decline overall since 1990. In 1994 mine production was 444.2 million ounces, down from the 514.2 million ounces produced in 1990. These production figures are likely to rise in future years. Silver production is primarily a by-product of gold and copper mining. If higher prices are in the cards for those metals, then expect silver production to rise. For silver to go substantially higher, industrial uses and investment will have to rise enough to outweigh any production increases.

Presently the main industrial uses for silver are electrical (37 percent of supply), photography (29 percent), and jewelry/silverware (27 percent). Physical silver sales for investment have waned in recent years, but they will probably pick up if metal prices start rising. Those who buy silver for investment these days do so primarily on the exchanges or options markets. (Hedgers and investors both prefer gold because it is less weighty and cumbersome.) Silver's average price is on the rise: $4.17 in 1992, $4.42 in 1993, and $5.28 in 1994.

Platinum

The fundamentals of platinum are much more interesting and encouraging than those of silver. The most striking feature is that over 90 percent of the supply comes from two unstable countries, South Africa and Russia. This situation lends itself to the possibility of supply disruptions that could have a crippling effect on certain industries—particularly the automobile industry—where platinum is used in catalytic convertors. At the same time, platinum is a minor cost component in auto production. Therefore, much higher prices presumably could be paid for platinum without having a major impact on auto prices. Over 40 percent of the platinum produced each year goes into catalytic convertors to control air pollution. As more and more countries modernize, governments impose pollution control restrictions that force the inclusion of catalytic convertors in automobiles. Another major component of platinum demand is for Japanese jew-

elry (32 percent). In 1994, according to Johnson Mat-
they, demand for platinum was up 11 percent to record
levels. Supply increased by only 3 percent.

Platinum has a tendency to outperform gold in bull
markets, but the downside is usually stronger as well.
Some estimate there is enough above-ground reserves
of platinum to last the industry less than two years.
This would be taken off the market in a short period
of time if an emergency were to crop up. An interrup-
tion in supply from either Russia or South Africa could
send platinum prices skyrocketing in a short period of
time. Another negative on the supply side is that most
Russian production occurs at the Noril'sk complex
deep in northern Siberia as a by-product of nickel
production. Labor problems and severe weather have
increasingly taken a toll on production. A similar situation exists in South Africa, where strikes, protests,
and the like have hampered production. Platinum
should be purchased not so much based on current
supply/demand tables, but instead on what the tables
would look like if one or both of these countries were
removed from the equation.

16

P is for...
Portfolio Planning: Putting It All Together

Essentially there are two broad categories of gold investors: those who want to hedge disaster and those who simply want to make a profit. There is a third type of investor who seeks to combine both objectives. Your needs will determine what you include in your portfolio. Some thought and attention must be given to which of the three categories you belong. Along these lines, if you place yourself in the "hedge disaster" category, you must also determine which economic disaster you consider most likely to occur—inflation, deflation, or both. What you decide in this respect will play a determining role in how your portfolio should be structured.

Portfolio planning is inherently a very personalized business. It cannot be done without strong input from the client. Do your homework. It is very important to the process. To plan your portfolio properly, consult with a professional. By that I mean, specifically, a

professional in the gold business. Stock brokers, financial planners, mutual fund sales personnel, and the
like have little knowledge of this highly specialized
field. As a result, they sometimes confuse more than
help. Quite often the course they recommend has
more to do with self-serving interests than with what
is best for the client. Below are some general guidelines for planning your portfolio. Those oriented toward hedging disaster generally prefer a combination
of gold bullion coins (Chapter 2) and pre-1933 $20
gold pieces (Chapter 20). The customary split is half
of each. The bullion coins are less expensive per
ounce of gold but are, or are likely to be, subject to
reporting requirements when you sell. They also
would be subject to confiscation if the government
were to prohibit gold. The $20 gold pieces are more
expensive per ounce of gold but provide relief from
government reporting and afford possible protection
against confiscation in exemptions that date back to
1933. If you rate the possibility of confiscation low
and are not concerned with reporting requirements,
then you should weight your portfolio in the direction
of bullion coins—anywhere from 60 percent to 100
percent. If you are concerned about confiscation and
reporting requirements, you should weight your holdings in the direction of $20 gold pieces—anywhere
from 60 percent to 100 percent.

If you want to design your portfolio for disaster
and potentially make profits, the process becomes
more complicated. Some combination of $20 gold
pieces, bullion coins, platinum, silver, and rare coins
is necessary. You should decide with the guidance of

an expert who can review with you the merits of each investment.

If you think you might need to use gold as money (Chapter 21), you should add 1/4-ounce bullion coins and/or pre-1933 U.S. $10 gold pieces that contain approximately 1/2-ounce of gold. These can be used for smaller transactions. An alternative, or addition, would be the $1,000 face value bags of pre-1965 silver coins that contain 715 ounces of silver and trade relatively close to the silver content.

If profit and profit alone is your main objective, bullion coins are the best alternative simply because the spread between the buying and selling is very close, within a few percentage points. Platinum and silver are also worth your consideration. Platinum has a history of outperforming gold in rising markets. Keep in mind that silver and platinum are primarily inflation hedges. They do not perform well in deflationary economies.

If you wish to hedge both inflation and deflation simultaneously, gold is your best bet. Gold tends to rise as the currency depreciates in inflationary times, while it tends to at least hold its value in deflationary times. Some analysts argue for much higher gold prices during deflation simply because gold is one of the few investments that would survive a massive debt default. This would generate unprecedented demand, which would drive prices higher.

If you feel inflation is the most likely future scenario, silver and platinum should be added to the mix. Another possibility for inflation hedgers is rare coins (Chapter 19) which have performed extraordinarily well during past inflationary episodes.

In any case, gold is the foundation of any precious metals portfolio simply because of its versatility. Whether to preserve assets or to make a profit, plan carefully under the guidance of a gold professional.

17

Q is for...
Quotable Notables on the Subject of Gold

Thousands of words have been written over the centuries about gold—some flattering, some not. Although the world has changed considerably since gold was first used as money in ancient times, the varied human reactions to gold haven't changed at all over the centuries. There are those who have understood and valued gold. Others have seen it as an impediment to their political and economic designs. Some have seen it as a symbol of greed, while still others have seen it as a symbol and instrument of freedom. Whatever the case, gold has indeed raised passions as well as a sense of practical security in the human soul, as noted in the following quotes supplied by the World Gold Council.

*There are about three hundred economists
in the world who are against gold,
and they think that gold
is a barbarous relic—and they might be right.
Unfortunately, there are three billion inhabitants
of the world who believe in gold.*
Janos Fekete (1912-)

Regardless of the dollar price involved, one ounce
of gold would purchase a quality man's suit at the
conclusion of the Revolutionary War, the Civil War,
the presidency of Franklin Roosevelt, and today.
Peter A. Bushre (1927-)

*There can be no other criterion, no other standard,
than gold. Yes, gold, which never changes, which can
be shaped into ingots, bars, coins, which has no
nationality and which is eternally and universally
accepted as the unalterable fiduciary par excellence.*
Charles de Gaulle (1890-1970)

Water is best, but gold shines like fire blazing in the
night, supreme of lordly wealth.
Pindar (522-443 B.C.)

*It is interesting to note that the average earnings of
an English worker in 1900 came to half an ounce of
gold a week and that in 1979, after two world wars,
a world slump, and a world inflation,
the British worker has average earnings
of half an ounce of gold a week.*
William Rees Mogg (1919-)

By common consent of the nations,
gold and silver are the only true measure of value.
They are the necessary regulators of trade.
I have myself no more doubt that these metals were
prepared by the Almighty for this very purpose,
than I have that iron and coal were prepared
for the purposes in which they are being used.
Helen McCulloch (1808-1895)

Although gold and silver are not by nature money,
money is by nature gold and silver.
Karl Marx (1818-1883)

Like liberty, gold never stays
where it is undervalued.
J. S. Morill (1810-1898)

Gold is not necessary. I have no interest in gold.
We'll build a solid state, without an ounce of gold
behind it. Anyone who sells above the set prices,
let him be marched off to a concentration camp.
That's the bastion of money.
Adolph Hitler (1889-1945)

The modern mind dislikes gold
because it blurts out unpleasant truths.
Joseph Schumpeter (1883-1950)

The tongue hath no force when gold speaketh.
Guazzo

Even during the period when Rome lost much of
her ancient prestige, an Indian traveler observed
that trade all over the world was operated with the
aid of Roman gold coins which were accepted and
admired everywhere.
Paul Einzig

As good as gold...
Charles Dickens (1812-1870)

You have to choose (as a voter) between trusting to
the natural stability of gold and the natural stability
and intelligence of the government.
And with due respect to these gentlemen,
I advise you, as long as the capitalist system lasts,
to vote for gold.
George Bernard Shaw (1856-1950)

It is extraordinary how many emotional storms
one may weather in safety
if one is ballasted with ever so little gold.
William McFee (1881-1945)

Though wisdom cannot be gotten for gold,
still less can it be gotten without it.
Samuel Butler (1835-1902)

Gold opens all locks,
no lock will hold against the power of gold.
George Herbert (1593-1633)

Gold were as good as twenty orators.
William Shakespeare (1564-1616)

Gold is a deep-persuading orator.
Richard Barnfield (1574-1627)

The balance distinguisheth
not between gold and lead.
George Herbert (1593-1633)

Gold is a treasure, and he who possesses it
does all he wishes to in this world,
and succeeds in helping souls into paradise.
Christopher Columbus (1451-1506)

In spite of all the romantic poets sing,
this gold my dearest is a useful thing.
Mary Leapor (1722-1746)

Gold is pale because it has
so many thieves plotting against it.
Diogenes (412-323 B.C.)

There can be no doubt that the international gold
standard, as it evolved in the nineteenth century,
provided the growing industrial world with the most
efficient system of adjustments for balance of
payments which it was ever to have, either by
accident or by conscious planning.
W. M. Scammell (1920-)

Not all that tempts you wandering eyes
And heedless hearts, is lawful prize
Nor all that glisten, gold.
Thomas Gray (1716-1771)

I could fill a volume with the many words, thoughts, and deeds surrounding gold. I think today's gold investors will appreciate these passages. Though times might change, the attitudes toward gold of both its defenders and detractors seem to remain the same.

18

R is for...
Reporting Requirements for Gold: What You Need to Know

There has been and continues to be a great deal of confusion about federal reporting requirements with respect to gold purchases and sales. Part of the problem results from the fact that it took the Internal Revenue Service almost seven years to publish regulations on gold reporting from the time they were required by the Tax Equity and Fiscal Responsibility Act. In addition, many gold brokers have an incomplete understanding of the regulations themselves and have often passed along the wrong information to gold investors. It took several years of negotiations between the Industry Council for Tangible Assets (ICTA) and the IRS just to get specific regulations published.

The following are reportable items as listed by the Internal Revenue Service. Also shown is the threshold number of ounces that triggers the need to file a Form 1099 with the IRS. Remember, the reporting require-

Gold bars (any size bars totaling 1 kilo—32.15 troy ounces—or more)	Gold Krugerrands (25 ounces or more)
Silver bars (1,000 ounces or more)	Gold Mexican Onzas (25 ounces or more)
Platinum bars (25 ounces or more); palladium bars (100 ounces or more) Gold Maple Leafs (25 ounces or more)	U.S. 90 percent silver coins, pre-1965 ($1,000 face value or more)

ment occurs *when you as a client sell, not when you purchase.*

Also, more than one transaction engaged in for the purpose of circumventing the reporting laws is to be treated as a single transaction. This includes transactions by more than one member of the same family. The 1099s also require the seller's Social Security number. The ICTA warns: "This information is provided to assist you and is not intended to be used by you as the sole guideline for complying with these regulations. You should consult your own tax professional...While a stricter interpretation of the regulations is possible, ICTA believes the above guidelines... fulfill the spirit of the negotiations and the intent of the Internal Revenue Service."

I feel obligated to pass along the same caveats. Much remains unclear with respect to these reporting requirements.

Although gold coins not listed above are now exempt from reporting, there is no guarantee they will be exempt in the future. On the contrary, since the intent of the law is to raise revenue, it is likely that coins not on the list now will be included in future regulations, especially if the gold price rises. In addition, it is possible for the same reasons that the number of coins required for the reporting threshold will be reduced as the price of gold rises. Remember, from the point of view of the U.S. Treasury, this is a revenue issue. For now, the best solution is to own at least half of your gold in pre-1933 $20 gold pieces. They have been exempted repeatedly from various regulations—including Form 1099 reporting requirements—because of their status as collectors' items. Finally, you cannot escape paying taxes on your gains simply because an item is not listed by the U.S. Treasury. You are still responsible for taxes on your gains whether or not the item falls into a reportable category.

The foregoing is meant to serve as an introduction to the reporting requirements for gold. The law and regulations are lengthy and complicated. If you are in doubt, the best course of action is to always discuss the matter with a tax consultant.

19

S is for...
Storing Your Gold

Gold and love affairs are difficult to hide.
—Old proverb

Most investors take possession of their gold and make their own storage arrangements. The following are the some of the most popular options.

Gold can be stored in a safety deposit box at your bank. This is the option most gold investors exercise. The downside of safety deposit boxes is that items are not insured against theft, fire, flood, or similar disasters. Another potential problem is, if the bank closes during a bank holiday, you many not be able to get to your gold when you most need it.

Another option is to store your gold at home or at the office in your own safe. Be careful here. I recommend a floor safe because it's easy to hide and difficult to crack. A freestanding safe, though, will also do the job. Insurance companies usually rate floor safes higher than freestanding safes, however. If you are thinking about storing gold at home, you might want to consult with a bonded safe company on the various options. You might also consider discussing the matter with your insurance agent before purchasing a safe. Your insurance company might offer coverage on your homeowner's policy. Some will cover gold, others won't.

Not always recommended, "midnight gardening"—burying gold on your property—is another option. There are storage canisters available that do not corrode when buried. When considering midnight gardening, keep in mind the story of the man who purchased a respectable amount of gold and buried it in his backyard. Several years later he sold the house but forgot about his buried gold. He had to make a commando raid in his old backyard in the wee hours of the morning to recover it. There have also been cases of children and widows of the deceased being unable to find buried gold.

In fact, I recall a couple instances in my career as a gold broker where I have had unusual calls about hidden gold. In one instance, a daughter called to say that she had reviewed several invoices for gold purchased by her father from my gold firm. Her mother was deceased as well, and before her father's death he had not told his daughter where he had hidden the gold. She hoped her father had disclosed the hiding place to me, and unfortunately he hadn't. In another instance a distraught wife who's husband was not a client of the firm, called to ask if I had any general ideas where somebody might store gold. He had purchased a large amount of gold and hidden it. He had suffered a stroke which paralyzed him and left him unable to speak. He could not tell her where the gold was hidden. Always leave instructions that can be easily found by your heirs as to where you have hidden gold, or disclose your hiding place to loved ones in case of unforeseen incidents.

If none of the options above suit you, the last option is to open an insured storage account at one of the depositories within the United States. Most of the top gold firms can refer you to a reputable storage facility. The insured storage option is particularly helpful to silver owners who do not wish to deal with the bulk and weight problems presented by silver. There are two types of institutional storage, fungible and nonfungible. *Fungible* storage means your gold is pooled with the gold of other depositors. There is no tagging or separation. *Nonfungible* storage means your gold is tagged and segregated. There is no pooling. Most gold owners prefer nonfungible storage because the specific coins they purchased will be sent to them when delivery is requested. With fungible accounts, there are more complicated procedures if you should request delivery. For this reason, they are avoided by investors who think they will someday want their gold in hand.

One of the advantages of insured storage is the ability to buy and sell over the phone. These features lend themselves well to individuals who travel but don't want the problems of receiving and storing precious metals. Most dealers, to avoid market exposure, will not set a price until they have received your metals in their own storage account or at their offices. The problem with insured storage is obvious. In case of an economic or other emergency, you might have difficulty getting your hands on your own metals for any number of reasons—natural disasters, communications shutdowns, social chaos, and the like.

Gold storage is not an easy problem to solve. You have to go with the option that best fits your needs and sense of safety.

20

T is for...

Twenty-Dollar Gold Pieces

> I am afraid that one day government will indeed call gold
> in. Gold bullion will be subject to confiscation. This is
> one big advantage to numismatic gold, such as Double
> Eagles (pre-1933 $20 gold pieces). It is an idiosyncrasy of
> governments that although they may prohibit ownership
> of gold in any form, they are reluctant to touch collections
> of numismatic gold coins.
>
> —Dr. Franz Pick

If gold is the immovable North Star of investments—
the center around which the universe of financial
assets rotates—then pre-1933 $20 gold pieces (Figure
16) are the solid foundation upon which the modern
gold portfolio is constructed.

Pre-1933 $20 gold pieces, which weigh nearly an
ounce of gold (.9675 ounce), track the gold price. At
the same time, they have been considered collector's
items by the government in many of the laws and
regulations concerning gold since their minting was
curtailed in the early 1930s. As a result, these items

offer a greater degree of privacy and latitude than the gold bullion coins. They also offer the best chance to escape gold confiscation—a possible source of concern for many gold investors.

How did this seemingly utilitarian coin, minted from the mid-1800s until 1933, come to play such a crucial role in planning today's gold portfolio? The story begins in 1933, when President Franklin D. Roosevelt called in the gold owned by the American people. In his confiscation order he likened gold to an invading army. "The private hoarding of gold and silver," said Roosevelt, "poses a grave threat to peace, equal justice, and the well-being of the United States." He referred to American citizens as "subjects of the United States" and ordered them to turn in their gold. All the safety deposit boxes in the country were sealed. Trading in gold was banned. Roosevelt publicly stated that Americans returning their gold to the government were participating in an act of patriotism that would help him deal with the devastating financial depression gripping the country. Privately, he knew that by confiscating gold, the government could set the value of the dollar without interference from the free gold market.

He claimed in subsequent years that he had never even read the confiscation order, that it was instead written by his advisors. It was one of the very first executive orders promulgated by a U.S. president. While criminalizing gold and (later on) silver bullion essentially as threats to the state, Roosevelt a few months later bowed to the hue and cry of gold advocates and exempted pre-1933 gold coins as collector's items. Attorney and gold advocate George Cooper had

this to say about the confiscation and the $20 gold
pieces:

> It is fairly clear that these items [pre-1933 $20 gold
> pieces] are protected under the Constitution's Fifth
> Amendment, which states "[N]or shall private
> property be taken for public use without just com-
> pensation." This is the well-known Eminent Do-
> main clause of the Constitution... What this means
> is that the individual can use the Eminent Domain
> clause to extract a "fair" price from the govern-
> ment for coins that are subject to confiscation...
> Roosevelt [in 1933] probably envisioned countless
> lawsuits clogging the court system just to deter-
> mine the value of someone's coin collection...
> thus the amendment to the executive order.

Keep in mind that the government's uppermost
purpose in the event of a confiscation is to block any
potential speculation against the currency. Pre-1933
$20 gold pieces do not represent a major threat be-
cause they make up such a small portion of the gold
supply. This heightens the likelihood they would be
passed over in a confiscation.

It is interesting to note that in Mexico restrictions
were placed on bullion ownership as the economy
deteriorated. Citizens could not own bullion or bullion
gold coins. They could own gold centennarios, 50-
peso gold coins containing 1.2 ounces of pure gold,
because the early dates had become collectors items.
Those who owned centennarios weathered the crash
nicely. Those who did not were devastated by the
December 1994 devaluation and the subsequent economic crash.

Figure 16

United States of America
$20 Gold Piece
Liberty Design
Gross Weight: 33.346 grams
Fineness: .900 or 21.6 karats
Diameter: 34mm
Fine Gold Content: .9675 ounce

United States of America
$20 Gold Piece
St. Gaudens Design
Gross Weight: 33.346 grams
Fineness: .900 or 21.6 karats
Diameter: 34mm
Fine Gold Content: .9675 ounce

Of the pre-1933 U.S. gold coins, the Liberty (minted from 1840 to 1907) and St. Gaudens (minted from 1907 to 1933) have become the most frequently traded because their prices are usually close to the bullion value while still being tagged as collectors' items. In the semi-numismatic grades (defined below), their value is greatly influenced by the gold price. The premium expands or contracts due to strengthening or diminishing demand. Historically, this has remained within a fairly tight range. In recent years, though, demand has picked up considerably. If the gold market turns bullish, the premium could skyrocket due to strong demand. As a result, there are two potential ways to profit from $20 gold pieces: either as the gold price rises or as the premium strengthens. The premium play pertains to uncirculated coins and is likely to be less pronounced in the circulated categories.

The coins trade in various grades, from the lower circulated grades through the higher uncirculated grades. *Grade* refers to the state of preservation, or quality, of the coin. In this section, the semi-numismatic grades from mint state 60 to mint state 64 are the subject of discussion. Once a $20 gold piece reaches the grade of mint state 65—a high degree of preservation—it then moves to the realm of pure numismatics. In this condition, rarity and market demand, not gold value, play the crucial role.

A rule of thumb: the higher the grade, the greater the spread between the gold value and the purchase price. The lowest grades *uncirculated* are the best way to go for individuals looking primarily for a gold investment. Because such a large percentage of the coin's price is related to gold value, the coin moves in tandem with the bullion gold price. This is an effective, low-maintenance approach to owning this type of gold. By purchasing mint state 60 or 61 coins, you reach your objective with respect to confiscation. At the same time, you maximize the amount of gold purchased per dollar invested.

If you go into the higher grades, mint state 62 and up, you get less gold for your money. However, you will have moved up the ladder in establishing yourself as a collector of gold coins, thus adding further insulation from potential gold confiscation. Whether this strategy fits any particular investor is a matter of discussion between the gold broker and the client in which the attendant risks are discussed, weighed, and analyzed. By going up the grading scale into the mint 62, 63 or 64 grades, you begin to move closer to the realm of numismatics where rarity begins to play an increasingly prominent role in value. It is important for you as an investor to understand the nuances between the two approaches. Determining the value of your gold usually entails making a call to your gold broker, who can tell you current values. The upside on these items is that they have double-play potential as both numismatic and gold items. The downside is that you get less gold for your money each grade you move up the scale.

Avoid the circulated grades unless you have assessed the risks in full and decide that the lower purchase price outweighs the possibilities of confiscation and of falling under the Internal Revenue Service's reporting requirements. The closer the coin trades to bullion value, the greater the risk the coin will be considered as a bullion item. With the circulated grades, investors sometimes find themselves selling at prices very near the net gold value and reporting requirements could apply.

If you purchase gold coins in the mint state 62 to mint state 64 grades, it is essential to have them graded and authenticated by one of the nationally accepted grading services, the Numismatic Guaranty Corporation (NGC) or the Professional Coin Grading Service (PCGS). Because the grading by these services is widely accepted around the country, you will increase your liquidity and the market for your coins when the time comes to sell. Independent grading is not crucial in purchasing the basic uncirculated coins (mint state 60 or 61) as long as you are purchasing them from a reputable gold firm. Because these coins trade more closely to the gold price, independent grading is a less crucial factor. You can purchase the lower-grade items graded if you prefer.

Keep in mind that not even this strategy of purchasing collectible gold will give you 100 percent protection from confiscation and government reporting requirements. However, you do have the weight of precedent in your favor. A large number of investors have already acquired these items in the hope that these precedents will carry the day.

As you can see, choosing the right coin could be a tricky business because there are a number of alternatives. St. Gaudens or Liberty? Graded by an independent service? Circulated or uncirculated? If uncirculated, which grade? Answers to these questions depend upon what you are trying to achieve. Choosing the right $20 gold piece is something you should do

in consultation with a gold professional who under-
stands what you are trying to accomplish.

Nearly every gold portfolio should contain a gen-
erous portion of pre-1933 $20 gold pieces. In most
portfolios, at least half the gold should be in this form.
You can also buy Liberty $10 gold pieces, which are
slightly more per ounce than the $20 gold pieces.
Those who buy the $10 gold pieces are usually think-
ing of using them as money in the event of a crash.

In the late 1920s, just prior to the stock market
crash, many of America's wealthiest investors purchased $20 gold pieces and shipped them to Europe
for storage. A huge hoard has existed there ever since.
As a result, most of the $20 gold pieces purchased by
today's investors are making their way back to the
United States from Europe. There is usually a waiting
list, as supply has been unable to keep up with demand in recent years.

The question is often asked whether the supply of
$20 gold pieces is likely to hold up. Some say the
supply is good and should last a long time. Others say
the supply is dwindling and it would be in your interest to accumulate as many as you can as quickly as
you can. It is a matter of common sense that we are
dealing with a finite supply. With the demand accelerating as it is, the supply will run out someday. The
best course of action at this time is to accelerate your
purchases until you feel you have enough. Then sit
back and see what happens. Owning gold is important. Owning the right kind of gold could be even
more important.

21

U is for...
Using Gold as Money

Since ancient times, gold has served humanity reliably as both a store of value and as a medium of exchange. Today, using gold as money seems completely out of place in a world moving toward the elimination of currency and its replacement with credit and debit cards and even cybernetic money. Yet the possibility of an economic crash has led many investors to put some gold away specifically for the purpose of buying essentials if the worst were to happen.

The smaller gold bullion coins (1/2, 1/4, and 1/10 ounce) best serve these purposes. Of that group, the 1/4-ounce coin is the most useful. Most of the countries that mint gold—including the United States, Austria and Canada—produce coins in the 1/4-ounce size. These are large enough to pass easily as currency from buyer to seller. They can be stacked, stored, and accumulated without the fear of losing a coin or two in the process—something that cannot be said for the smaller, 1/10-ounce coin. The premium is slightly higher on the 1/4-ounce coin (over the 1-ounce coin) because the cost of making a coin is roughly the same no matter the size. The cost is amortized over a larger amount of gold in the 1-ounce coins, hence the difference percentage-wise.

Those concerned with confiscation and privacy matters might consider owning the uncirculated $10 Liberty coins as a medium of exchange. The $10 Liberty approximates 1/2-ounce of gold. Since there are no reporting requirements on this item, you can purchase goods without either you or the seller having to be concerned about federal reporting requirements.

In addition to the above recommendations, you might want to consider a bag or two of silver ($1,000 face value, pre-1965 U.S. silver coins). The old standard recommendation has been one bag per family member living with you. This still stands. U.S. silver dollars are still recommended occasionally for this purpose, but the premium is relatively high. The greatest advantage of silver dollars is that they fall under the 1933 dateline with respect to confiscation. Silver rounds of various manufacture are another alternative. Again, the premium is higher for the rounds than the bags, and these could be subject to confiscation.

Having money to barter could be crucial during an economic breakdown. It makes sense to have some gold and silver put away for this purpose. This is not a complicated problem. This advice should suffice in the event of a breakdown.

22

V is for...
Vital Statistics

Chemical symbol for gold = Au

Atomic weight = 196.967

Specific gravity = 19.32

Tensile strength = 11.9

Estimated mine production = 100,000+ tons since gold was first discovered

Atomic number = 79

Melting point = 1,063 degrees

Hardness (Brinell) = 25

Occurrence of gold in the earth's crust = .005 parts per million

First gold coin = minted by Croesus of Lydia about 560 B.C.

   Gold is one of the densest of all the chemical elements. It is the most malleable metal. One ounce of gold can be drawn into a wire about thirty-five miles long. Gold is chemically related to copper and silver.

It is highly resistant to chemical change and cannot be dissolved in common acids. Gold does dissolve, however, in aqua regia and cyanides.

Weights & Measures

1 troy ounce = 31.1034 grams
1 troy ounce = 480 grains
1 troy ounce = 20 punts
3.75 troy ounces = 10 tolas (Indian Subcontinent)
6.02 troy ounces = 5 taels (Chinese)
32.15 troy ounces = 1 kilogram
32,150 troy ounces = 1 metric ton (1,000 kilos)
1 troy ounce = 1.0971 ounce avoirdupois (U.S.)

Standard Bar Sizes

400 troy ounces (12.5 kilos)
32.15 troy ounces (1 kilo)
100 troy ounces (3.11 kilos)

Also, a wide variety of smaller-sized bars by various manufacturers are not deliverable to any exchange, but trade among makers in smaller markets.

Carat Gold Conversions

24-carat = .995 to .9999 pure (fine) gold
22-carat = .916 pure (fine) gold
18-carat = .750 pure (fine) gold
14-carat = .583 pure (fine) gold
10-carat = .4167 pure (fine) gold

23

W is for…

What Should I do and When Should I Do It? A Sensible Gold Strategy for the Rest of the 1990s

Forecasting the gold price is at best a risky and complicated undertaking. As a result, for most inventors, the key to successful gold investing will not come from predicting the price on a short-term basis, but in implementing a strategy which takes advantage of gold's well established long-term behavior.

The most telling aspect of this behavior is characterized by the spikes that dominate the long-term gold chart (See Figure 17). Gold has a tendency to remain flat over extended periods of time for a variety of economic and political reasons (which we will not cover in this section), then break to the upside peaking usually at multiples of its starting point. Taking advantage of these spikes is difficult from a timing point of view but there is a strategy which makes good sense given the circumstances.

Figure 17. London Gold, Average Price

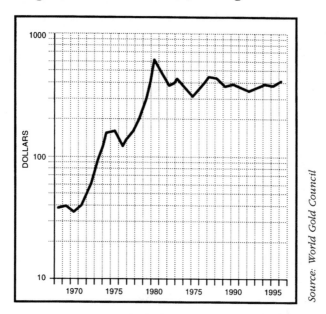

Source: World Gold Council

From 1933 to 1971, there was little reason for private gold ownership because the dollar was gold-backed. This changed in 1971 when Richard Nixon severed the link between the dollar and gold and set the dollar free to fluctuate against the world's other major currencies. Then, gold became a matter of interest not only for American investors but investors around the world. With the dollar no longer backed by gold, currencies free to fluctuate against each other, and gold released to seek its free market level, a whole new era for the gold market was ushered in. During the 1970's the gold price spiked on two occasions. In 1974 it reached the $200 level—an almost sixfold increase from the $35 benchmark bottom. After retracing to the $100 level in 1976, it spiked again in the late 1970's peaking at $875—almost nine times its bottom price. In Figure 16, the average annual gold price is graphed on the logarithmic scale to show the comparable, relative strength of the two spikes. On a standard chart the 1974 spike is shown to be nearly the equal of the 1979 peak. The logarithmic chart also emphasizes the range-bound gold price of recent years—a circumstance from a technical point of view some analysts have equated to the $35 to $42 price range that preceded the 1970's bull market.

Is the current trading range signaling another spike to the upside? Chances are that it is, though as we said, predicting when the move will begin is difficult. The best strategy will take advantage of gold's historical price behavior, i.e. its tendency to spike. It is difficult for investors to take advantage of these spikes through short-term instruments like futures contracts, options on futures, bank leverage programs and even to a certain extent gold stocks simply because it is so difficult to predict when the spikes will occur. If a leveraged investor were to get lucky and catch a spike, the returns would be phenomenal, but the odds weigh heavily against this happening. Statistics show that 85 percent of all investors in futures and options lose money. That percentage is probably higher with leveraged gold investments.

Instead the best way to take advantage of the gold's price behavior is through a long-term accumulation program of the physical metal itself, where you buy, take delivery and store for the upcoming spike. A sophistication of this strategy would be to divide your gold holdings in half—one part comprising a core holding to be held long term against the possibility of a currency collapse, stock market crash, or economic calamity and the other to be sold off for profit. Given the nature of gold, this strategy to accumulate and hold makes good sense for the remainder of the 1990s and fulfills the needs of most gold investors.

24

X is for...
The XYZs of Gold Investing: Some Final Thoughts

The case for gold ownership in the modern era rests on two fundamental premises. First, in the absence of a gold standard, there is no discipline on the issue of paper currency. As a result, individuals would be well served to put themselves on the gold standard through private gold ownership as a means to preserve their assets. Second, the sound fundamentals of gold—particularly the wide gap between international usage and mine production—will ultimately push the price upward. The second assumption has been well developed in this book. Let me make one last elaboration on the first.

Throughout this book I have tried to offer the kind of practical advice I would provide a client who asks for it. I have tried to picture myself sitting with a potential gold buyer and answering the typical questions he or she would ask. Buyers always want to know what's going to happen with the gold price. I always tell them that if I knew what was going to happen with gold, I would mortgage myself to the hilt and put it all into gold. But I *don't* know what's going to happen with gold in the short run. Neither does anybody else. We have a good idea what's going to happen over an extended period of time based on historical analysis, the fundamentals and so on. But in the short run, just about anything can happen. And it usually does.

Markets, if anything, are a humbling experience. Even the best analysts are usually wrong more times than they are right. With gold, the best advice, as I have proffered more than once in this book, is to buy and accumulate over the medium- to long-term. Gold is primarily insurance against the proverbial rainy day. Beyond that, if we should benefit as investors from a spike in the price, consider it a bonus. Do not go into a gold investment with stars in your eyes. Fast and sure returns are not gold's mission in the overall port-folio. Safety and asset preservation are.

The graphs that follow (Figures 18 and 19) illus-trate the point. History has shown that whenever the gold backing for paper money is removed, inflation ensues. This is no less true in the United States than it has been in countless other countries throughout mod-ern history. Whenever government management of the currency plays a critical role in its value, that value is eventually undermined, diminished, and finally de-stroyed.

The first graph (Figure 18) contrasts the gold standard years, 1900 to 1971, versus the era of the fiat dollar standard, 1971 to the present. Gold showed remarkable stability when it was the centerpiece of the world's monetary system. As a result, the dollar and inflation were also stable. The dramatic upsurge in the gold price came after the gold backing was removed from the dollar in 1971 and the government was free to conduct monetary and fiscal policy without the discipline of the gold standard. Inflation rates jumped aggressively, and so did gold. The dollar's rapid depreciation since 1971, when the gold backing was removed (Figure 19), is equally revealing. From 1971 to today, the dollar has lost 73 percent of its purchasing power and is now worth 26 cents based on the Labor Department's consumer price index. Even in recent years when the inflation rate has moderated, the effects on the purchasing power of the dollar have been more than one would presume. It surprises people to know that the 1980 dollar is now worth 55

Figure 18. Gold Price: Gold Standard versus Paper Dollar Standard

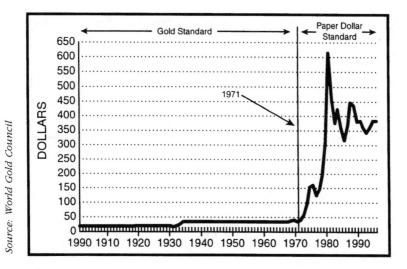

Source: World Gold Council

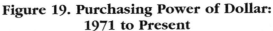

**Figure 19. Purchasing Power of Dollar:
1971 to Present**

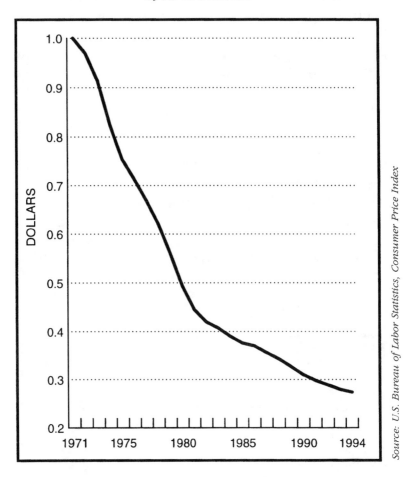

Source: U.S. Bureau of Labor Statistics, Consumer Price Index

cents. In other words, despite the claims of government economists to the contrary, the debasement of
the dollar continues even in these years when inflation
is supposedly under control. From time to time, financial historians talk about the ongoing war against gold

waged by the central banks of the world, particularly by the United States. Unfortunately, this has not just been a war against gold; inadvertently, it has also been a war against the dollar, as the two charts display. It is a war that *over the long run* gold is winning and the dollar is losing. No one really knows when the final curtain will fall on the dollar, but we do know that signs of deterioration abound.

Few Americans know that in 1945 the gold reserve of the United States amounted to 22,000 tons, over 50 percent of the world's above-ground stock and the largest hoard on earth. Now the U.S. Treasury's gold reserve stands at a little over 8,000 tons, or 8 percent of the world's total. Most of that gold was expended to defend the dollar's role as the centerpiece of the international monetary system. For this we have paid a dear price. In less than a decade and a half, the United States has gone from being the greatest creditor nation on earth to being the greatest debtor nation on earth. It has lost 65 percent of its gold stock and has watched its currency slide into the abyss. Our standard of living has suffered as a result. At one time 70 percent of the world's gold reserves were held by governments and their central banks, with the U.S. Treasury holding the single greatest portion. Now 70 percent of the gold is in the hands of private individuals worldwide. Ironically, they hold it as security against the potential breakdown of the dollar-based international financial system. At the same time, many of the world's central banks, perhaps because they sense danger, are in a dollar reduction mode. A decade ago, dollar reserves amounted to 90 percent of the world's currency reserves. Today they amount to 50 percent. In 1999 Europe will introduce its own reserve currency that will likely supplant the dollar on that continent.

Although all of this bodes well for the gold price, it does not bode well for the United States and the dollar. The nation must get its financial house in order. If it doesn't, the challenges to the dollar will continue with potentially even more punitive and unfortunate results. In the meantime, a diversification into gold by American investors makes a great deal of sense. History is on the side of the yellow metal. Given the situation, it is a matter of common sense and financial prudence to prepare for the worst and hope for the best.

I hope this book serves as a means to an end for those of you who are interested in gold and need a basic education on the subject. You are now prepared to incorporate gold into your portfolio. Gold should provide you with a little peace of mind in an era of increasing uncertainty. If this book should contribute to that end, then it has served its purpose.

Appendix I
Newsletter Review

The following list of newsletters covers not only gold but also the social, political, and economic issues pertinent to gold ownership. Most are published monthly. Addresses are provided so that you may contact the publishers if you have an interest. A short comment is included to give you some idea of the each newsletter's approach and its scope of coverage. This list is in no way intended to be a complete list of all newsletters reporting on gold.

Barron's
The Dow Jones Business and Financial Weekly
200 Burnett Road
Chicopee, MA 01020

Published weekly, this publication offers economic data as well as the financial news and easy-to-read market reports. For this reason it is a valuable info source for gold investors even though its focus is on the equities markets. The columnists are good, particularly Randall W. Forsythe who is quoted frequently in newsletters. Also, this newspaper has been balanced in its treatment of gold, something that cannot be said for all financial publications. This newspaper is excellent source of information.

The Big Picure
Stephen Leeb, Ph. D., Editor
1750 Old Meadow Road
Suite 301
McClean, VA 22102

A top analyst, Leeb believes that the current economic situation can only resolve itself in another round of inflation. He suggests inflation hedges, including gold, and offers stock picks in nearly every issue to benefit from his analysis. A good part of his analysis comes from an intuitive sense of what's going on at the Federal Reserve.

Crawford Perspectives
Arch Crawford, Editor
1382 Third Avenue, Suite 403
New York, NY 10021

Market timing by planetary cycles and technical analysis since 1977. Formerly head of research at Merrill Lynch, Arch Crawford is highly respected in the newsletter industry. *Crawford Perspectives* is usually among the highest-rated newsletters with respect to timing the stock and gold markets. Monthly gold section. Technically oriented.

Dow Theory Letters
Richard Russell, Editor
P.O. Box 1759
La Jolla, CA 92038

Russell is one of the deans of the newsletter business. Forthright. Doesn't mince words. Practical approach to markets. One of the originators of the Dow theory approach to markets. Covers the stock market and gold each month. Bullish on gold for the long term. Combination of fundamentals, technicals, and common sense. Often quoted by other letter writers.

The Elliott Wave Theorist
Robert Prechter, Editor
P.O. Box 1618
Gainesville, GA 30503

Highly respected technical analysis using the theories and works of R.N. Elliott. Called the stock market crash of 1987. Believes we are on the verge of a stock market crash and a major depression. A must for left-brain dominant, analytical types.

Freemarket Gold & Money Report
James Turk, Editor
P.O. Box 4634
Greenwich, CT 06830

One of the most highly regarded newsletters focusing on gold. A good blend of both scholarly and more practical approaches. A good source for inside news on the gold market. Highly recommended.

Freedom Daily
Jacob C. Hornberger, Editor
11350 Random Hills Road
Suite 800
Fairfax, VA 22030

Deep thinking on economic and political problems of the day. Libertarian/conservative. Historical perspectives for current problems. For those who miss the days when

William F. Buckley had other things on his mind than sailing.

The Free Market
Llewellyn Rockwell, Editor
c/o The Ludwig von Mises Institute
Auburn, AL 36849
The definitive newsletter for libertarian thinking. Where the late economist Murray Rothbard was published. Articles by top thinkers in the libertarian movement. Includes book reviews. Basically a political/economics letter. In-depth analysis issue by issue.

Financial Privacy Report
Michael Ketcher, Editor
P.O. Box 1277
Burnsville, MN 55337
The best newsletter on privacy issues confronting Americans today. Covers one subject in depth each month. Not afraid to tell it like it is.

Financial Trend Forecaster
Timothy McMahon, Editor
2929 Amherst Highway
Madison Heights, VA 24572
Publisher of the *Moore Financial Indicator*, the widely followed predictor of the inflation rate. Bullish on gold. Discusses the effects of inflation on various investment markets.

Fuller Money
David Fuller, Editor
7 Swallow Street
London, W1R7HD
United Kingdom

Technical analysis from the other side of the pond. Covers all markets, including gold, currencies, and international stock markets. Excellent commentary. Good source for gauging attitudes in Britain and Europe. Quite often referred to by other newsletter writers as having a level-headed, down-to-earth approach to the markets.

Gold Demand Trends
World Gold Council
900 Third Avenue
New York, NY 10022

The widely used reference and analytical tool on gold demand worldwide. Used mostly by industry professionals. No political or economic commentary. Published quarterly.

Gold Newsletter
James U. Blanchard, Editor
2400 Jefferson Highway
Suite 600
Jefferson, LA 70121

One of the top gold letters from one of the original goldbugs.

Gold Survey (Annually since 1968)
Gold Fields Mineral Services (GFMS)
Greencoat House
Francis Street
London SWP 1DH
United Kingdom

The annual survey of GFMS, supplemented by twice-yearly interim Updates, is regarded as the most authoritative analysis of gold supply and demand. It covers all aspects of the physical and paper markets, including the impact of producer hedging and central bank activities on the market.

Harry Schultz Letter
Harry Schultz
PO Box 622
CH-1001
Lausanne, Switzerland

Harry's been around for a long time, in his own words, "for thinking humanoids." An unabashed goldbug.

Inside View
David Hall, Editor
1936 E. Deere Avenue
Suite 102
Santa Ana, CA 92705

Information on investing in rare coins from one of the top dealers in the field including hot picks, what to avoid and what to buy, and in-depth numismatic analysis.

Investment Analyst
Adrian Day, Editor
1217 St. Paul Street
Baltimore, MD 21202
One of the largest circulation newsletters in the United
States. Very bullish on gold and gold stocks. Also discusses international markets and activities of traders in
the gold market. Has a knack for zeroing-in on meaning-
ful statistical developments in the economy and markets.

The Money Changer
F. Sanders, Editor
P.O. Box 341753
Memphis, TN 38184

In-depth political and economic analysis as it relates to
the gold market. Newspaper format. Packs a great deal
into each issue. If you are looking for intelligent discussion on everything from supply/demand stats on gold to
an analysis of E-money, this letter will hold your interest.

Money-Forecast Letter
Adrian Van Eck, Editor
1750 Washington Street, P.O. Box 8006
Holliston, MA 01746
Covers the Federal Reserve Bank and issues surrounding
it. Likes gold and real estate. Been around a long time.
Gives good historical background on money issues affecting us today. One of the better Fed watchers. Info
delivered in a style non-economists will appreciate.

Myers' Finance Review
John Myers, Editor
P.O. Box 467939
Atlanta, GA 31146

Easy-to-read approach to complex issues, including good graphs, charts, etc. Very good on gold and issues affecting its price. In-depth treatment of economic problems like the deficit, declining dollar, etc. Tells good, highly readable stories about friends and family that always carry a "financial moral."

News & Views
Forecasts, Commentary and Analysis on the Economy and Precious Metals
Michael J. Kosares, Editor
3033 E. First Avenue
Suite 407
Denver, CO 80206

A digest of the news and views of various newsletter writers on subjects ranging from gold to the economy to the political situation. Includes a good section on a wide range of items in a quick-read format called "Short & Sweet." A good way to get a great deal of information on the gold market from one source.

Otto Scott's Compass
Otto Scott, Editor
P.O. Box 69006
Seattle, WA 98003

This newsletter represents what's best in the newsletter publishing business. Each issue centers on a single subject that is treated in depth. Highly respected by his peers, Scott offers clear, conservative thinking that usually sheds new light on the subjects treated. Also writes movie and book reviews which transcend what you usually read in your local newspaper.

Past Present Futures
James Flanagan, Editor
606 Wilshire Boulevard
Suite 402
Santa Monica, CA 90401

Technical and fundamental analysis of the commodities markets. Helpful with market timing and singling out strong indicators of future trends.

Precious Metals Digest
Dennis Wheeler, Editor
P.O. Box 467939
Atlanta, GA 31146

Reprints and analysis from a number of other newsletters. Focus on gold, silver, and platinum. Recommends mining issues. Good, reliable information source. Always on top of the gold market.

The Steve Puetz Letter
Steve Puetz, Editor
2800 Wilshire Avenue
W. Lafayette, IN 47906

No-nonsense analysis of all the markets. Believes stock market crash and depression are inevitable. Predicts gold will go to $5,000 during a currency meltdown, contraction, and crash. Scholarly. Solid information. Great charts that drive home his point. For the thinking investor.

John Pugsley's Journal
John Pugsley, Editor
23-00 Rt. 208
Fair Lawn, NJ 07410
Thoughts and advice from one of America's top analysts.

The Reaper
R.E. McMaster, Jr., Editor
P.O. Box 84901
Phoenix, AZ. 85071
One of the better all-around newsletters. He covers everything from commodities markets to sun spot cycles. One of the top experts on the gold market. Never dull. Often controversial. Combines market terminology and philosophy. Intellectual and challenging. Has an intuitive sense of the markets that others lack.

Richard Maybury's Early Warning Report
Richard Maybury, Editor
P.O. Box 84908
Phoenix, AZ 85071
Probably the best geopolitical/strategic letter now being published. Maybury has his finger on the pulse of developments in what ne calls Chaostan—the geographic region encompassing Eastern Europe (including Russia), the Mid East and western Asia. He sees war on the horizon and rush to hard assets including gold. If you are looking for international geopolitical analysis that goes beyond the evening news, Maybury provides it.

The Richebacher Letter
Dr. Kurt Richebacher, Editor
1129 E. Cliff Road
Burnsville, MN 55337
Ex-banker from Germany's largest bank. Excellent information and interpretation of economic trends. Good information on the international banking community and central bank activities. A must for the advanced student of international monetary trends. This is the letter central bankers read.

The Ruff Times
Howard J. Ruff, Editor
P.O. Box 700
San Lorenzo, CA 94580
Interesting social commentary and investment recommendations from one of the deans of the newsletter business. Author of several investment bestsellers during the 1970s and 1980s.

Silver & Gold Report
James DiGeorgia, Editor
P.O. Box 109665
Palm Beach Gardens, FL 33410
He offers advice on gold and silver, including what to buy and what not to buy.

Strategic Investment
Rt. Hon. Lord Rees-Mogg &
James Dale Davidson, Editors
824 E. Baltimore Street
Baltimore, MD 21202

In-depth analysis of all the markets. Economic and political journalism which quite often makes the front
pages of the country's newspapers. This newsletter is
intelligent and useful not just for its investment advice
but for its commentary as well.

The Ron Paul Survival Report
Ron Paul, Editor
P.O. Box 602
Lake Jackson, TX 77566

The best political newsletter available. Mr. Paul is a
Texas congressman. Conservative/libertarian approach.
Analysis of the Beltway from someone who knows the
ropes. Gold-oriented. Mr. Paul formerly served on the
U.S. House Banking Subcommittee.

The Wall Street Underground, Inc.
Nick Guarino, Editor
1129 E. Cliff Road
Burnsville, MN 55337

Holds nothing back. Concerned about insider manipula-
tions of various markets, including stocks and gold. The
fastest growing newsletter in the United States. Currently
recommends 30 percent portfolio diversification into
gold.

The Van Eck Gold And Mutual Fund Advisory
Jonathan Van Eck, Editor
1750 Washington Street
Holliston, MA 01746

Solid commentary and analysis of the gold market, including supply/demand fundamentals and the political forces that drive the market. Recommends gold and specific gold stocks.

Appendix II
Historical Gold Prices
London's Gold Bullion Market
Yearly Average Price

1900	18.96	1916	18.99	1932	20.69
1901	18.98	1917	18.99	1933	26.33
1902	18.97	1918	18.99	1934	34.69
1903	18.95	1919	19.95	1935	34.84
1904	18.96	1920	20.68	1936	34.87
1905	18.92	1921	20.58	1937	34.79
1906	18.90	1922	20.66	1938	34.85
1907	18.94	1923	21.32	1939	34.42
1908	18.95	1924	20.69	1940	33.85
1909	18.96	1925	20.64	1941	33.85
1910	18.92	1926	20.63	1942	33.85
1911	18.92	1927	20.64	1943	33.85
1912	18.93	1928	20.66	1944	33.85
1913	18.92	1929	20.63	1945	34.71
1914	18.99	1930	20.65	1946	34.71
1915	18.99	1931	17.06	1947	34.71

1948	34.71	1964	35.10	1980	615.00
1949	31.69	1965	35.12	1981	460.00
1950	34.72	1966	35.13	1982	376.00
1951	34.72	1967	34.95	1983	424.00
1952	34.60	1968	39.31	1984	361.00
1953	34.84	1969	41.28	1985	317.00
1954	35.04	1970	36.02	1986	368.00
1955	35.03	1971	40.62	1987	447.00
1956	34.99	1972	58.42	1988	437.00
1957	34.95	1973	97.39	1989	381.44
1958	35.10	1974	154.00	1990	383.51
1959	35.10	1975	160.86	1991	362.11
1960	35.27	1976	124.74	1992	343.82
1961	35.25	1977	147.84	1993	359.77
1962	35.23	1978	193.40	1994	384.00
1963	35.09	1979	306.00	1995	384.17

Source: World Gold Council

Bibliography

To distill almost twenty-five years of study in the fields of economic philosophy, political science, history, and social theory as they relate to gold is a difficult, if not impossible, undertaking. The following book references and monographs contributed directly and *concretely* in one way or another to this book. I owe their authors a debt of gratitude. In addition, the list is meant to give some direction to those interested in a more contemporary discussion on gold and its role in modern society and the international economy.

Gold:

Caldwell, Taylor. *Great Lion of God.* New York: Ballantine Books, 1970.

Goldfields Mineral Services, Ltd. *Gold 1996* and *Gold 1996 Update I.* London, 1996.

Green, Timothy. *The Gold Companion.* Great Britain: Rosendale Press, 1991.

Green, Timothy. *The New World of Gold.* New York: Walker and Company, 1984.

Jastrum, Roy. *The Golden Constant.* New York: John
Wiley & Sons, 1977.

Jenkins, G. K. *Ancient Greek Coins.* New York: G. P.
Putnam & Sons, 1972.

Nichols, Jeffery. *How to Profit from the Coming Boom
in Gold.* New York: McGraw-Hill, Inc., 1992.

Turk, James. "Do Central Banks Control the Gold
Market?" *Freemarket Gold & Money Report,*
Greenwich, Ct., 1994.

World Gold Council. *The Gold Borrowing Market: A
Decade of Growth.* Prepared by Ian Cox. Geneva.

World Gold Council. *Gold Demand Trends, A
Quarterly Publication.* New York: 1996.

World Gold Council. *Globalization and Risk
Management: Selected Papers from the Fourth City of
London Central Banking Conference.* Geneva, 1995.

World Gold Council. *The Management of Reserve
Assets: Opportunities and Risks in a Multi-Currency
System.* Prepared by Dr. H. J. Witteveen. Geneva,
1993.

General Reference:

*Barron's, The Dow Jones Business and Financial
Weekly.* Chicopee, Ma., 1996.

Grun, Bernard. *The Timetables of History: A Horizontal
Linkage of People and Events.* New York: Simon &
Schuster, 1991.

U.S. Department of Commerce. Economics and Statistics Administration. *The Statistical Abstract of the United States: National Data Book.* Washington, D.C., 1995.

U.S. Department of the Treasury. *Treasury Bulletin.* Washington, D.C., 1996.

Index

About the Author

Michael J. Kosares is the founder and president of Centennial Precious Metals, one of the oldest and most prestigious U.S. gold firms serving private gold investors. The company is located in Denver, just a stone's throw from Cherry Creek, where gold was first discovered in 1858. For the past twenty-five years, Kosares has counseled gold investors from all walks of life. He and his wife Nancy and their two children, Jonathan and Andrea, make their home in Denver.

Kosares is also editor and publisher of the widely read newsletter *News & Views: Analysis, Forecasts, and Commentary on Precious Metals & the Economy.* Free sample subscriptions are available from Centennial Precious Metals. Or, for quotes or information about gold and other precious metals, write or call:

Centennial Precious Metals
3033 E. First Avenue Suite 407
Denver, CO 80206
Ph. 1-800-869-5115

Web site: USAGold.com

Please send:

The ABCs of Gold Investing

___	Copies at $14.95 each =	_____
	Nebraska residents add 5% sales tax	_____
	Shipping & handling: $4.00 for first book $1.00 for each additional	_____
	Total Enclosed	_____

Name _____

Address _____

City _____ State ____ Zip _____

Phone ( ) _____

(Please clip or photocopy above section)

Send check or money order to:

**Addicus Books
P.O. Box 45327
Omaha, NE 68145**

Or, order toll free: 1-800-352-2873

Visit the Addicus Books web site:
www.AddicusBooks.com

Quantity Purchases

Organizations, associations, corporations, colleges and other groups may qualify for special discounts when ordering more than 24 copies of *The ABCs of Gold Investing*. Please specify quantity desired. Write or call Special Sales Department, Addicus Books, P.O. Box 45327, Omaha, NE 68145.